Differentiated Instructional Strategies
for Reading in the Content Areas

Differentiated Instructional Strategies
for Reading in the Content Areas

Carolyn Chapman • Rita King

CORWIN PRESS, INC.
A Sage Publications Company
Thousand Oaks, California

For information:

Corwin Press, Inc.
A Sage Publications Company
2455 Teller Road
Thousand Oaks, California 91320
www.corwinpress.com

Sage Publications Ltd.
6 Bonhill Street
London EC2A 4PU
United Kingdom

Sage Publications India Pvt. Ltd.
B-42, Panchsheel Enclave
Post Box 4109
New Delhi 110 017 India

Printed in the United States of America

Library of Congress Cataloging-in-Publication Data

Chapman, Carolyn, 1945-
Differentiated instructional strategies for reading in the content areas /
Carolyn Chapman and Rita King.
      p. cm.
Includes bibliographical references (p.   ) and index.
ISBN 0-7619-3824-9 (cloth) — ISBN 0-7619-3825-7 (paper)
   1. Content area reading. 2. Language arts—Correlation with content subjects.
3. Individualized instruction. I. King, Rita M. II. Title.
LB1050.455.C52 2003
372.41´6—dc21

                                                              2003005246

This book is printed on acid-free paper.

03   04   05   06   10   9   8   7   6   5   4   3   2   1

Illustrations by Tammy Kay Brunson and Richard Venard Willis

Acquisitions editor:	Faye Zucker
Editorial assistant:	Stacy Wagner
Production editor:	Sanford Robinson
Copy editor:	Pam Suwinsky
Typesetter:	C&M Digitals (P) Ltd.
Proofreader:	Toni Williams
Cover designer:	Tracy E. Miller
Production artist:	Lisa Miller
Indexer:	Teri Greenberg

Dedication

To our Mothers,
Closs Pickren Mizell and
Louise Long Schaerer.

These dedicated teachers
opened up our world to the love of books and
made a difference in the reading life of every child they taught.
Their influence led us to become readers, writers and educators.
They instilled in us the determination, zeal and passion
to make a difference for readers of all ages.

To students who are struggling
to become comprehending readers.
To teachers who are committed to giving students
the lifelong gift of reading.

Contents

Every teacher knows that some students struggle to read their texts while others go unchallenged. Every teacher who wants to be a facilitator of learning must therefore also be a facilitator of reading. Differentiated reading instruction gives teachers in all subject areas the power to help students succeed at all ability levels. It is never too late to help students become confident, eager, and fluent readers and to move students toward their full reading potential.

An inviting, safe, and accepting classroom environment promotes optimal learning experiences. To motivate learners with diverse reading abilities, teachers can create print-rich environments, comfortable reading spots, and a wide variety of unique and differentiated celebrations when reading and learning goals are met. Attention to the affective realms of learning—rapport, empathy, challenge, excitement, humor, respect, choice, self-efficacy, and more—marks those teachers who become legends in learners' lives.

The effective teacher in the differentiated reading classroom assesses each learner's reading behaviors, feelings toward reading, reading skill levels, developmental readiness for reading, and diverse needs. Diagnostic tools, possible problems, and suggested solutions can be differentiated for emerging, successful, and fluent readers. Checklists, surveys, and rubrics can be used to assess multiple intelligences, thinking styles, learning styles, 4Mat types, personal characteristics, beliefs, and interests.

The effective teacher in the differentiated reading classroom selects and adapts instructional models that coordinate reader needs with content standards and learning objectives. Models of reading include Adjustable Assignments, Curriculum Compacting, centers and projects, Independent Choice, Guided Reading, Shared Reading, Language Experience, Read Aloud, and Four Block. Also included are strategies to support those models, such as agendas, cubing, response books, graphic organizers, and choice boards.

A teacher may say, "I taught that word!" but that is not the same as the student asking, "Did I learn that word?" In the differentiated reading classroom, the teacher uses stimulating, novel, and meaningful strategies to introduce new words essential to reading experiences and assignments in the content areas. Included here are more than fifty strategies for vocabulary learning, vocabulary visuals, context clues, and assessments that can connect new words to the learner's world and help the learner take ownership of new subject vocabulary.

No other aspect of the language arts curriculum has received as much attention as phonics. This chapter offers twelve key phonics skills and essential word analysis skills covering syllables, root words, prefixes, and suffixes. These skills can be infused across the curriculum while teaching content area vocabulary.

Differentiated comprehension strategies can be used to meet the diverse interests, ability levels, and background knowledge levels of each learner. Included here are strategies and assessments to use before, during, and after reading. Find flexible grouping designs for Total groups (T), reading Alone (A), Partner reading (P), and Small groups (S).

Variety is the spice of learning, and teachers who vary their strategies, assessments, and homework assignments empower their students to become successful readers both inside and outside the classroom.

Acknowledgments

The authors extend a warm thank you to the following educators who have assisted and inspired us through our writing of this book: Liz Bennett, Marti Richardson, Terri Stumpf, Joan Clark Mann, and Jane Poole.

A special thank you to the faculty of Davies County High School in Owensboro, Kentucky, the middle school teachers of Dekalb and Richmond Counties in Georgia, and the summer course participants in Knoxville, Tennessee. These teachers implemented many of these strategies across the content areas and gave us encouraging feedback during the writing of this book.

We express deep appreciation to Douglas Rife, Anita Linton, and Faye Zucker of Corwin Press for their support and belief in our passion to make a difference for educators and students through our writing.

Jim Chapman continuously praised, encouraged, and supported us during this project. Jim is "our rock". His patience continually sustains us. He is our number one listening ear and cheerleader.

Corwin Press thanks the following reviewers for their contributions to this volume:

Marsha Riddle Buly, Bellingham, WA
Nancy Creech, Roseville, MI
Anita Davis, Spartanburg, SC
William Fitzhugh, Reisterstown, MD
Ann Fulk, Fairfax Station, VA
Robin Smith, Buckingham, VA
Debbie Wilks, Wichita, KS

About the Authors

Carolyn Chapman continues her life's goal as an international educational consultant, author, and teacher. She supports educators in their process of change for today's students. She has taught in kindergarten to college classrooms. Her interactive, hands-on professional development opportunities focus on challenging the mind to ensure success for learners of all ages. All students *do* learn. Why not take control of that learning by putting excitement and quality in effective learning? Carolyn walks her walk and talks her talk to make a difference in the journey of learning in today's classrooms.

Carolyn authored *If the Shoe Fits . . . How to Develop Multiple Intelligences in the Classroom.* She has co-authored *Multiple Assessments for Multiple Intelligences, Multiple Intelligences Through Centers and Projects, Differentiated Instructional Strategies for Writing in the Content Areas, Differentiated Instructional Strategies: One Size Doesn't Fit All,* and *Test Success in the Brain Compatible Classroom.* Video Journal of Education, Inc., features Carolyn Chapman in Differentiated Instruction. Carolyn's company, Creative Learning Connection, Inc., has also produced a CD, *Carolyn Chapman's Making the Shoe Fit,* and training manuals to accompany each of her books. Each of these publications and her trainings demonstrate Carolyn's desire and determination to make an effective impact for educators and students. She may be contacted through the Creative Learning Connection Web site at www.carolynchapman.com.

Rita King is an adjunct professor in the Department of Educational Leadership at Middle Tennessee State University. She has more than twenty years of teacher-training experience. As principal and director of the university's teacher-training program in the laboratory school, she taught methods courses and conducted demonstration lessons. Rita's doctorate degree is in Educational Leadership. Her formal training (Ed.D, Ed.S., M.A., and B.S.) has been directly related to education and teacher training.

As an international consultant, Rita conducts training sessions for teachers, administrators, and parents on local, state, and international levels. Her areas of expertise include multiple intelligences, practical applications of brain-based research, differentiated learning, reading and writing strategies, creating effective learning environments, and strategies for test success. Rita's sessions give educators and parents innovative, engaging activities to develop students as self-directed, independent learners. Participants enjoy Rita's practical, easy-to-use strategies, sense of humor, enthusiasm, and genuine desire to foster the love of learning.

Rita co-authored *Test Success in the Brain Compatible Classroom* and *Differentiated Instructional Strategies for Writing in the Content Areas.* She also coauthored training manuals to accompany professional development trainings for *Differentiated Instructional Strategies: One Size Doesn't Fit All, Differentiated Instructional Strategies for Writing in the Content Areas,* and *Differentiated Instructional Strategies for Reading in the Content Areas.*

Rita may be contacted through Creative Learning Connection or kingrs@bellsouth.net

INTRODUCTION
Infusing Reading in the Content Areas

Every teacher who wants to be a facilitator of learning (Readence, Bean, & Baldwin, 1998) must also be a reading teacher, because reading is an essential component of learning in every subject. All teachers know that some students in their classrooms struggle to read their texts while other students go unchallenged. A learner's reading difficulties become more apparent with the challenges of increasingly complex texts and materials in the content areas as he moves through the grade levels; that student must receive help to develop the skills and strategies he needs in order to succeed in school and in life.

SAILING INTO DIFFERENTIATED READING INSTRUCTION

Differentiating instruction for reading is similar to the preparation needed for a sailing adventure. The captain identifies each crew member's specialty and talent so that assignments can be made in his area of expertise to make the journey a success. Likewise, each reader has unique skills and talents as well as the right to learn all the information he possibly can. For this to occur, reading experiences and learning experiences must be personalized and individualized during the reading journey.

Teachers are the captains who set the course for the reader's journey, deciding how each one will travel and what each will learn along the way.

Differentiated instruction for this kind of smooth sailing toward learning and accomplishment in the content areas must be based on effective pre-assessments of the learner's knowledge, skills, and abilities. It must be student-centered, with active learning, and flexible enough to meet the changing needs of all readers.

Don't you wish you could wave a magic wand that could turn every student in your classroom into a fluent, comprehending reader? At the current time, we have too many readers who struggle to read their texts so they can complete assignments. We also have too many readers who are unchallenged. But we don't have a prepackaged, magic formula to teach our students to read. However, teachers do have the power to create strategies that work for readers of all ability levels by using differentiated instruction. Every teacher can use the ideas in this book to meet the needs of readers at all levels, because it is never too late to move a reader toward his reading potential.

Early childhood teachers are teaching balanced literacy programs that include effective systematic reading activities. Teachers are using an interesting variety of literature-based materials. The programs emphasize skills for comprehension, vocabulary development, and phonics. Writing as a process is strategically integrated with these programs. Differentiated instruction provides teachers with strategies and models that incorporate these quality teaching approaches while meeting the diverse needs of readers.

Too much valuable time is expended blaming former teachers, parents, textbook companies, and curriculum programs for the reader's problems. If this time and energy is used productively to assess and diagnose the student's reading ability, the information can be used to design reading lessons for successful learning experiences. Teachers need to use every opportunity to improve their students' reading ability. The learner's smallest improvement has the potential to create a miraculous change in his life. Each teacher needs to remind himself daily of the role he plays in each student's successful reading journey.

A student's self-doubt must be transformed from "I don't think I can . . . " to "I know I can . . . !" Effective teachers are aware of each opportunity to assist a learner and encourage him to reach his reading potential. The quality of a student's life often depends on his reading ability.

THE GOALS OF THIS BOOK

The goals of this reading book are to meet the unique learning needs of each reader through differentiated instruction. This book includes:

- Reading activities that empower students in vocabulary development, phonics, and comprehension

- Learning strategies designed to be infused in subject-related texts and supplementary materials
- Assessment ideas to quickly diagnose the reader's problems, along with suggested prescriptions for solutions
- Memory strategies that are easy for a reader to apply as he processes information for long-term memory
- Techniques and tips to assist teachers as they establish an effective learning environment that is conducive to reading

All of our strategies, activities, and ideas are designed to infuse basic reading skills in content areas. They are designed for teachers to adapt to the needs of individual readers so that teachers can make a difference in each learner's academic and personal endeavors.

All aspects of this resource are grounded in brain-based research that provides the rationale for the strategies and approaches used. The research includes effective practices related to establishing the learning environment (Bruer, 1994), understanding the reader's problems, and finding solutions.

The authors hope this book meets its primary goal to assist teachers with the infusion of differentiated reading strategies into daily lessons across the curriculum. We hope the activities intrigue, challenge, actively engage, and empower each struggling student to become an eager, confident, and fluent reader.

ESSENTIAL QUESTIONS

Essential questions stimulate higher-order thinking. The questions give the individual time to combine his ideas, to elaborate on the topic, and to evaluate the situation. Here are some probing questions that are related to a struggling reader's problems:

Are the student's inadequate comprehension skills the result of poor word identification and vocabulary strategies? Often the student has not mastered the skills needed to become a fluent reader. If he has not learned the basics of reading, he will have difficulty reading.

Does the student's inability to understand texts and related information exist because he has not mastered basic comprehension strategies? It is not unusual to have a student who reads fluently but is unable to mentally process written material. He does not comprehend or remember information. Another learner calls words but does not understand basic sentence structure. Yet another student may recall facts but find it difficult to get the "jist" or to summarize. The student needs a repertoire of comprehension strategies and skills to apply automatically as needed.

Figure 0.1 Tools and strategies for infusing reading in the differentiated classroom

Creating the Climate	Knowing the Reader	Models of Reading	Vocabulary	Art of Decoding	Comprehension

Environment
• Safe
• Non-threatening
• Challenging
• Nurturing
• Stimulating
• Positive
• Motivating
• Comfortable
 	
Materials
• Print-rich
• Ready Resources
 	
Tone
• Celebration
• Excitement
• Acceptance
 	
Provide Choices
• Choice Boards
 	
Self- Efficacy Assessment
• Checklists
• Surveys
	Meet the Reading Characters
	• Emerging Emily
	• Word-Calling Wayne
	• Insecure Inez
	• Turned-Off Tom
	• Correcting Carl
	• Read Aloud Renee
	• Silent Reading Sam
	• Comprehending Carlos
	
	Assessment and Diagnosis of Readers
	• Behaviors
	• Feelings of the Reader
	• Diagnosis
	• Possible Solutions
	
	Multiple Intelligences
	• Gardner
	
	Learning Styles
	• Sternberg
	• Gregory
	• McCarthy
	• Object View
	
	Assessment
	• Checklists
	• Surveys
	• Inventories
	• Conferences
		Differentiated Instructional Models
		• Adjustable Assignment
		• Curriculum Compacting
		• Centers and Projects
		• Problem Solving
		
		Reading Models
		• Independent Choice Reading
		• Guided Reading
		• Language Experience
		• Shared Reading
		• Read Aloud
		
		Classroom Design
		• Four Block
		  ➤ Vocabulary Development
		  ➤ Independent Reading
		  ➤ Guided reading
		  ➤ Writing
		
		From Models to Instruction
		• Agendas/Menus
		• Cubing
		• Response Books
		• Graphic Organizers
		• Choice Boards
			Personal Ownership
			• Sight Words
			• Word Discovery
			• Word Mastery
			• Base Words
			
			Teaching the Word
			• Motions
			• Box it!
			• Beats
			• Illustrations
			• Puzzles
			• Games
			• Humor
			
			Analyze the Word
			• Word Attack
			• Antonyms
			• Synonyms
			• Compound Words
			• Analogies
			
			Vocabulary Visuals
			• Walls to Vines
			• Personal Collections
			
			Word Meaning
			• Clues
			• Cues
			
			Assessment and Diagnosis
			• Miscue Analysis
			• Master Multiple Meaning
			• Checklists
			• Informal Reading Inventories
			• Cloze Process
				Phonics Instruction
				• Role
				• Debate
				
				Phonics Rules
				• The Phonics Dozen
				
				Structural Analysis
				• Root words
				• Base words
				• Prefixes
				• Suffixes
				• Syllabification
				• Accent Cues
				• Structural Cues
				
				Assessment
				• The Phonics Dozen Checklist
					Levels
					• Literal
					• Inferential
					• Evaluative
					
					Reading an Assignment
					• Passage Preview
					• Passage View
					• Passage Review
					
					Flexible Grouping Designs
					• **T** Total Group
					• **A** Alone
					• **P** Partner
					• **S** Small Groups
					
					Vary Genres and Formats
					
					Effective Questioning
					
					Assessments
					• Checklists
					• Running Record
					• Portfolios
					• The Grading Dilemma

4

Is the learner capable of reading and comprehending the material, but lacking in motivation to use the skills and strategies to read? Often a comprehending reader lacks the desire to read. He is "turned off" as a reader by boring, lengthy assignments. This occurs when he has little interest in topics, or when assignments have no link or connection to his personal world. Students read the information they want to read. A motivated reader needs a purpose, an interest, and the desire to read.

A major role of the teacher is to fuel and sustain the student's desire to read and to learn. The teacher stimulates and guides the learner until this desire becomes an internal force. When the student is motivated, he becomes a responsible, self-directed, fluent reader. In the learning journey, the student needs this internal drive to reach his reading potential. Thrust is a must!

EFFECTIVE PRACTICES AND RELATED RESEARCH

This book presents strategies, activities, and techniques to improve the performance of all readers. Varied assessments, diagnostic tools, and strategies are emphasized. All methods and approaches are based on the most current research and effective practices related to teaching and learning. The following brain-based research is the supporting information used to improve reading comprehension skills in the strategies, activities, and ideas. Other research is interwoven and cited throughout the book.

Schema Theories

Schema theories state that new information is constructed to fit information currently existing in the mind. When a teacher introduces a topic, each student has a different schema or mental picture that is a result of prior knowledge and experiences. The new information must be presented so that learners "fit" the new learning with their schemas. The ideas existing in a student's mind organize and create meaning from new experiences. This is the reason it is important to understand and use students' prior knowledge and experiences to plan effectively for new learning (Piaget, 1952).

Constructing New Knowledge

Learners play a major role in constructing new knowledge. Vygotsky's and Piaget's work in the later part of the twentieth century emphasized the value of the individual student's role in the learning process.

Four major components of Vygotsky's and Piaget's theories (Kauchak & Eggen, 1998) are

1. Learners construct their own knowledge.

2. Prior knowledge is the foundation for new learning.

3. Social interaction enriches learning experiences.

4. Authentic learning generates personal meaning.

Memory Lanes

Marilee Sprenger (1999) points out that new information enters the brain through the senses. She identifies at least five pathways that carry information into memory. The following explanations of each pathway may be adapted to teach readers at all grade levels the strategies they can use to remember information.

Semantic:	Understanding the meaning and purposes
Episodic:	Recalling events, specific episodes, and happenings
Procedural:	Using the steps or sequence
Automatic:	Practiced, learned, and mastered
Emotional:	Feelings

As you develop lesson plans, identify the memory pathway readers will use to store and retrieve the information during specific activities.

Strategy Ownership

Strategy construction is the discovery of a procedure to use for processing information. The student needs to connect key information with his prior knowledge and know how to apply it to other problems or situations (Siegler, 1998).

Intriguing strategies help the reader to learn, apply, store, and retrieve information. Strategies are easier for a student if they are presented in his favorite ways to learn. Select and design strategies for the student to apply independently as needed. The learner will "own" a strategy when he knows how to use it automatically. When the reader takes ownership of a learning tool, he possesses it for his personal use for a lifetime.

DIFFERENTIATION

We define the term *differentiation* as a philosophy that enables teachers to plan strategically in order to reach the needs of diverse learners in classrooms today (Gregory & Chapman, 2002a; Chapman & King, 2003).

Differentiation meets learners "where they are" in their ability and offers challenging, appropriate options for them to achieve success.

Differentiation shows respect for learner differences. Everyone comes from different experiences and bring different emotions to the learning situation. Not only does the learner have to have the desire to learn, he has to be ready for the information, understand the learning purpose, and see where it fits in his unique mind.

Differentiate the Content

Educators now realize that students need to learn as much as they possibly can on their own ability levels. It is true that there is no cap on potential, so if a learner knows the information, he needs to move to a portion of the topic where he can learn about it. The repetition of previously learned information wastes time for the learner. When information is repeated, the student often becomes bored and unmotivated.

Some students are ready for the content that is planned and taught. Many times, these learners are the target of the teacher's plans. In most classrooms, the same information is taught using texts, materials, and terms on varying levels of difficulty.

Students no longer need to learn the same information at the same time. If the content is too difficult or above the student's reading ability level, it is easy for him to become frustrated and turned off to learning. This student often experiences the "I can't" feeling. He has missed some of the pieces he needs to move ahead to the content information he is expected to learn.

Differentiate Assessment Tools

Use a variety of assessment tools to obtain an accurate diagnosis of the learner's needs.

Pre-assessment

In order to meet the diverse needs of the learner, conduct a pre-assessment two or three weeks prior to the teaching of the information (Gregory & Chapman, 2002a). Use the pre-assessment data when planning strategically to meet the needs of individual students in the group.

Informal Assessment During Instruction

Informal assessment tools are quick and easy. Often they tell the way the student feels about the information. For example, when a teacher asks a student to show a "thumbs up" if he understands what is being taught, a "thumbs to the side" signal if he is grasping some of the information, or a "thumbs down" if he does not have a clue, then the teacher knows immediately just where the student is with his understanding of the concept being taught. If the environment is set for students to know they can reveal misunderstandings, a teacher can provide the necessary resources needed for understanding.

Formal Assessments: Performance Evidence

Various collections of performance evidence can be used. Portfolios reflect learners' independent progress. Sometimes it is necessary to administer a more formal assessment to measure knowledge base and areas of need. In this case, a pretest can be given before the lesson to target strength and weak areas in the learning. If the same pretest is given to everyone, no one should make a perfect score, but everyone should be able to answer some of the questions. The test should address the needs of those who do not know much about the information as well as those who are experts on the topic. When the same posttest is given at the end of the study, it will measure knowledge growth and learning accomplishments.

Differentiate Performance Tasks

If I can think it, I can say it
If I can say it I can write it!
If I can write it, I can read it.
If I can read it, I can decide if I need it.
If I need it, I can decide where and how I can use it!

—Chapman and King, 2003

It is crucial to examine how well the student performs a task or shows what he knows or demonstrates how he will use the information. Reflection and evaluation is complete with words or print. Identify the student's understanding by asking him to choose from a list of options how he will demonstrate what he has learned. Encourage the student to use his creative abilities to complete the task. Examples of performance assessments:

Role-playing	Demonstrations	Explanations	Musical creations
Graphic organizers	Posters	Read Alouds	Pictures

Differentiate Instructional Strategies

Plan assignments so that students are actively engaged in the learning. Each learner needs to experience challenges, choices, and success as he strives to reach his learning goals.

Vary instructional strategies so individual needs can be met for unique learning styles, modalities, and intelligences. Standards target expectations and give a plan for teaching content. The art of teaching is in knowing how to teach to each one. How the standards are taught is up to each individual teacher. Use a variety of strategies to teach a concept.

Provide a relaxed reading environment where students become investigators, researchers, and discoverers. This builds opportunities for reading success. Students need high-level, interesting reading materials to be challenged. Everyone has a way of reading materials and remembering information. Reading experiences need to accommodate these needs.

Recognize each reader's likes, dislikes, strengths, and weaknesses. Build on the reader's likes and strengths, and strengthen his weaknesses. If a student knows the material, he should be allowed to show what he knows in a way that he chooses.

Give students as many choices as possible. Understand the reader, and provide appropriate experiences within his range of success. Allow students to work independently in centers or workstations.

Make the reading event an exciting happening in the learning journey. Give the students opportunities to use the information they have learned. Open the door! Remember that an enemy of understanding is covering material instead of aiming for in-depth understanding. Give everyone's unique brain a true variety of experiences.

THE READING JOURNEY

When sailboats leave the shore, they usually have a destination. Often several vessels depart at the same time on their way to a predetermined place. Each craft takes its own course, because the sea is a big place and there are many routes to the chosen destination.

Curriculum is planned within units of focus because the brain works by making links and connections. The information to be learned during the journey is established, but the components introduced, taught, and explored in each classroom will vary. The standards, goals, and objectives for a given topic may be the same, but each journey will be unique. This is true from class period to class period, from teacher to teacher, and from year to year. The route of the learning journey depends on many factors, including the information presented, student and teacher interests, and prior learning experiences.

The Captain and Crew

The captain maps the course to the destination. Throughout the trip there are changes to the plan that require problem solving and decision making.

Each crew member on board is assigned specific jobs or roles. Some individuals are more experienced than others; they may train rookie crew members. Teams work together to complete many tasks. Often crew members need to work independently. The captain remains at the helm and oversees the crew's duties and responsibilities.

The Teacher and Students

Like the captain, the teacher guides the learning journey. The curriculum format is planned, classroom decisions made, and goals established. Each student's talents, experiences, interests, and prior knowledge are considered, because each individual is a distinct and unique member of the crew for the learning journey. Each student is responsible and accountable for his own learning. Class members have various roles including learner, friend, and teacher in daily school routines. The teacher is aware of the way each learner approaches a task, problem, or situation. As the student learns something new, he adds experiences to his prior knowledge base and increases his intelligence.

The Teacher as the Captain of the Reading Journey

The teacher is a leader, mediator, facilitator, advisor, boss, and friend. Throughout the journey, the teacher:

- Assesses each crew member's abilities and needs
- Plans the trip and designs the curriculum
- Establishes rules and guidelines
- Interviews each crew member
- Obtains background information on each crew member
- Uses a variety of methods to learn about the reader
- Works the crew, knows their emotional hooks
- Uncovers crew members' talents by observing and surveying
- Conferences with the crew
- Determines the resources needed for the journey
- Makes final decisions: May get help from the crew
- Changes or adjusts the course as needed
- Evaluates each crew member's success
- Sets the destination for the next excursion
- Establishes new team roles or maintains and revamps previous responsibilities as needed
- Uses differentiated instructional strategies to work smarter, not harder

The Students Are the Unique Crew

Students are thinkers, doers, risk takers, problem solvers, and inquirers. They take on responsibility and have a passion for learning. Throughout the journey, the students:

- Go about their individual tasks through self-direction
- Solve task-related problems in their way to get the job done well
- Apply their strengths and talents
- Work well with others and recognize their talents
- Contribute to the crew's success
- Learn from successes and mistakes

Assessing the Crew

Individual crew members report to the captain and receive feedback when things are going right or wrong. Often the captain doesn't assess the surroundings accurately or does not listen to or heed the danger signals from the crew. The *Titantic*'s captain thought his ship would never sink. He was experienced but did not pay attention to the warnings or the new, correct information. The use of a different maneuver would have placed the ship on another course and saved the vessel. The teacher must be knowledgeable about a variety of strategies and be flexible so a different approach can be taken as needed. Needs cannot be ignored. Various assessment strategies can be used for a deeper understanding of needs and to make changes in direction. The teacher as the captain is in charge and makes the final life-changing decisions for the reader's success or failure.

Assessing and Revamping the Curriculum Plan

When teachers fail to plan, they plan to fail. The teacher designs the curriculum plan. Sometimes students do not understand the information, and their needs become obvious. When these signals indicate a need for review or reteaching for understanding, the students need a new way to work with the materials. During the learning journey, students become interested in particular topic areas. The teacher can take advantage of these learning opportunities and add experiences to meet the learner's desire to fulfill his curiosity. Differentiated instruction provides a variety of strategies for deeper individual understanding and extended learning opportunities.

Staying on Course

When the destination at sea is not visible, the captain and crew find ways to keep moving toward the direction. They do not give up. They navigate their way to the predetermined goal. Hazards such as storms, high winds, or wave turbulence may hinder the sailing vessel and extend the journey. Rerouting may be necessary to avoid obstacles. When stormy seas appear, the captain may reduce the speed or change routes. He may need to lower the anchor beneath the surface of the water to decrease the vessel's speed. It may be necessary for him to lower the anchor to the sea floor for temporary repairs.

Many sailboats complete their excursion on calm seas without being deterred and have no need to make changes in the original plans. Smooth sailing with a "Full speed ahead" signal is the ideal experience.

Teachers chart the course for the reader's learning journey. When readers have difficulty with a concept or skill, the teacher directs them to the set goals by using a variety of learning strategies, materials, and resources. It may take longer to reach goals and objectives, but the extra time involved in learning a skill will be worth it when the reader knows how to apply it and the skill becomes the foundation for new learning. Some readers reach established goals with very little assistance. This type of independent learning is the mission of educators.

SUMMARY

Educators now have the methods, strategies, and materials to assist students in their individual academic excursions in school and throughout life. No longer can we teach to students in the middle ability range and hope that all the other students will receive something from the information. Learning experiences must match the many ways students learn. The adage "One size does not fit all" reminds us that a major paradigm shift is needed for optimal learning to take place.

Creating a Climate for Reading 1

The classroom environment has a major impact on student motivation. The teacher's genuine interest and high expectations for students are key elements in the atmosphere of the reading classroom. The students' attitudes toward reading and learning are influenced by the energy and enthusiasm exhibited by the teacher.

An inviting classroom environment promotes learning. Strategically planned activities provide optimal learning experiences, and all efforts of the learner are supported in a non-threatening, comfortable environment.

MOTIVATING LEARNERS WITH DIVERSE READING ABILITIES

The differentiated reading classroom shows respect for learner differences. Students bring different experiences and different emotions to their learning situations. Not only does the learner have to have the desire to learn, he has to be ready for the information, understand the learning purpose, and see where it fits in his unique mind.

Students with Diverse Reading Abilities

Students have a wide range of reading abilities. Each individual has unique physical, emotional, social, and academic needs. Many students have reading skills far below the grade level of the text and supplementary materials. Struggling readers may bring to the classroom diverse cultural and economic backgrounds. Teachers are expected to meet the needs of these struggling, reluctant readers as well as those of the enthusiastic, talented readers.

Often a learner's negative attitudes toward reading are the result of his experiences with past failures. In the primary grades, a child uses easy, reader-friendly texts and fictional materials. Adult assistance and guidance are available. As the reader moves through the grades, however, books and factual materials become more complex and difficult. The student is expected to complete learning tasks independently. A reluctant reader may not succeed because he constantly struggles with comprehension of the factual texts and supplementary grade-level materials. A capable reader may not reach his reading potential because he continually struggles with boring, unchallenging material. To meet the needs of all learners, the teachers must present stimulating and engaging lessons on all the readers' ability and interest levels.

How do teachers find time to teach basic reading skills and strategies to these diverse learners when they are required to teach the subject standards, skills, and objectives effectively? They infuse reading strategies in novel and engaging ways with topic-related information. This challenges and motivates students to *want* to read. The student's focus remains on the content information.

Teachers Who Become Legends in Learners' Lives

Everyone knows a legend—the teacher who is successful at bringing out the best in students, regardless of the location of the school, the diversity of the students, the conditions of the facilities, or the availability of resources.

—Scheidecker and Freeman, 1999

A teacher becomes a legend in students' lives by showing genuine care and concern for the pupils' well-being. A teacher's daily interest in his students may change the direction of their lives. Struggling readers require nurturing. Students need to know someone cares and will meet their specific needs. Learners live up to high expectations when they want to please their teacher. When a learner's strengths are emphasized and when a success is praised, those become small steps toward permanent change in that student's education journey.

The differentiated reading classroom is an environment that reflects the teacher's joy of learning information in a subject. The student reader observes the teacher's daily enthusiasm and interest in lessons through the evidence exhibited in presentations, daily routines, body language, and conversation. The student is molded by the teacher's belief in his ability and by the teacher's high expectations.

MOTIVATING LEARNERS IN THE DIFFERENTIATED READING CLASSROOM

William Glasser's Choice Theory of Motivation (Glasser, 1990, 1998) cites five important student needs for learning motivation. Carol Ann Tomlinson's *Parallel Curriculum* (Tomlinson et al., 2002) also names five motivating needs that can be incorporated when inviting students to learn. Figure 1.1 adapts the views of Glasser and Tomlinson to the reading classroom.

Figure 1.1 Needs for reading motivation

Glasser's Needs	Tomlinson's Needs	The Effective Classroom Culture Provides the Reader with . . .
To survive and reproduce	Affirmation	Basic needs Acceptance A meaningful place in the learning culture Membership in a group
To belong and be loved	Contribution	Experiences that make a difference Opportunities to make contributions to the class A nurturing environment Acceptance A risk-free environment Freedom for expression
To have freedom	Purpose	Exploration and discovery Opportunities with decision making and problem solving Self-efficacy
To have power	Power	Opportunities to make decisions Choices Active learning Understanding of purpose, directions, and goals Empowerment
To have fun	Satisfaction	Challenges to stimulate the mind Activities of interest Choices Work in comfort zones Active learning Humor and fun

Metacognition

Metacognition in reading, according to Peterson and VanDerWege (2002), involves a turning inward—at first purposefully and later automatically—to examine how we comprehend a text. Teachers need to model these self-monitoring techniques (Honig, 2001).

We define the term *metacognition* as "knowing about knowing." When a learner "knows that he knows" a reading skill or strategy, and "knows that he knows" how to use it, he becomes a more responsible, effective reader. A struggling reader needs to see metacognitive strategies modeled. He needs to hear the "inside" thinking that accompanies the procedures, so he can "think about his thinking" as he practices the skill. Conscious oral practice leads to automatic applications. Readers become successful when they can apply needed skills and strategies automatically.

Flow

The state of *flow* occurs when a learner is doing something that occupies and stimulates his mind (Csikszentmihalyi, 1990). For instance, when he reads something that he wants to read, he may read for a long time and not realize that anyone else is around. He is so focused on the information or the activity that he is unaware of his surroundings. During this time, he is in a state of flow.

So many times students go through an entire school day and never experience the state of flow. Teachers can identify a student's state of flow through observation, inventories, surveys, and conversations. Use this information in lesson planning to capture the reader's attention and interest.

It has been shown with recent studies of magnetic resonance images (MRIs) and the workings of the brain (Sousa, 2001) that after a person is engaged in the state of flow, during the next activity the learner participates in, no matter how difficult, he performs better and his ability to concentrate is heightened.

A CLASSROOM ENVIRONMENT THAT MEETS READERS' NEEDS

The reader–environment fit is determined by the influence of the physical and perceptual factors in classrooms. The physical aspects include the seating and furniture arrangement, visuals, and temperature. The perceptual factors include the teacher's presence, expectations, personal interactions, and the feelings generated by the surroundings in the learning climate. According to Caine and Caine (1994), "The skill in good teaching lies in the capacity to orchestrate the sensory context of the class." This orchestration includes meeting the students' physical, emotional, social, and academic needs.

Design a Print-Rich Environment

Design a comfortable, personalized place for the student to read. Colorful, high-interest bulletin boards, posters, charts, mobiles, and displays reflect the information taught. Involve the student in setting the stage for learning, so he will have a sense of ownership and belonging. For example, ask the students to design a pictorial timeline or story sequence around the classroom walls to create a colorful border. The students' pride in the designs becomes evident, and the classroom comes alive with the displayed information. Provide a print-rich environment by asking students to prepare display materials using the information taught. Create attractive galleries with student work so learning becomes visible reflections of the objectives and standards.

Supply Ready Resources

One of the teacher's greatest challenges is to provide ability-level resources and materials that are interesting and intriguing to the student. Select materials to match the student's ability and knowledge level. Include related fiction and nonfiction books as supplementary resources. Establish a section of the room with these materials for the readers. Provide various reading materials, including books, periodicals, reference materials, computer programs, and other resources. Remove outdated materials that are not useful to the class members.

Give students time to brainstorm suggestions for materials to add to the resources. This will generate a list of materials the students want and are interested in reading. Challenge readers to add materials to the resource center throughout the semester. Encourage students to discover places in public, at school, and at home where they can read to get information. Provide "free choice" time for students to browse and read the selected material. This gives students a sense of ownership and personalizes their learning experiences (see Figure 1.2).

Create an Ideal Reading Spot

Provide cozy and comfortable places to read. If possible, allow students to choose where they want to sit to read.

Create Novel Spaces for Readers. Examples:

Bean bag	Stool	Couch	Rocking chair	Boat
Tree house	Loft	Bench	Stationary bike	Rug
Sleeping bag	Tent	Cot	Beach towel	Lounge chair
Glider	Swing	Carpet square	Hammock	Treadmill

Figure 1.2   Reading: Here, there, everywhere

Public	School	Home
• Signs	• Charts	• Labels
• Advertisements	• Reports	• Brochures
• Billboards	• Graphs	• Headlines
• Labels	• Directions	• Letters
• Newspapers	• Captions	• Bills
• Store signs	• Maps	• E-mail
• Street names	• Glossaries	• Web sites
• Movie reviews	• Instruction sheets	• Comic strips
• Books	• Rules	• Catalogs
• Magazines	• Manuals	• Recipes
• Maps	• Indexes	• Calendars
• Banners	• Diagrams	• Reviews
• Score boards	• Schedules	• Notes
• Brochures	• Posters	• Directions
• Tags	• Diaries	• Newspapers
• Traffic signs	• Books	• Magazines
• Menus	• Signs	• Manuals
• Schedules	• Displays	• Postal mail

Supply Props for the Reading Corner. Examples:

Sunglasses	Artifacts	Reading lamp	Lantern
Flashlight	Pin light	Stuffed animals	Magnifying glass
CD player	Tape recorder	Hats, caps,	Background
Earphones	Goggles	or helmets	music

Celebrate Reading Achievements

Read-a-Book Celebrations

For each book read:

- Place a marble in a large glass jar.
- Write the name of the book and the author and student's critique on a card to display.
- Add a candle to a cake.
- Add a spot on a leopard.
- Place a button on a bear.
- Place a sticker in a class book.

- Add a page to the class diary of reading reviews.
- Place the name, author, and review on a book shape and hang it on a string for a book clothesline.
- Decorate a door, hallway, side of a cabinet, or bulletin board with reading lists or critiques of completed books.

Project Displays

Display the projects in an area for others to learn the information and appreciate the reader's efforts and creativity. Display places may include:

- Classrooms
- Media centers
- Cafeteria walls
- Stages
- Entrances and exits
- Boxes
- Ceiling tiles
- Hallways
- Foyers
- Columns
- Bathroom walls

Project Designs

- Dioramas
- Models
- Posters
- Mobiles
- PowerPoint presentations
- Galleries
- Scrapbook albums
- Videos
- Photographs
- Character museums
- Puppet theaters
- Theatrical performances
- Trifold posters with related objects displayed
- Recordings with earphones
- Multimedia presentations

Unique Celebrations When Reading Goals Are Met

When a class or school meets a reading goal, something completely unique can be planned as a crazy celebration. If a teacher or a member of the school staff performs one of the following actions, the students will experience a day that rewards and celebrates reading while also creating memories that connect exciting experiences with reading.

- Sit on the school roof for a day in a lounge chair with an umbrella, book, and picnic basket of goodies.
- Perform a favorite song.
- Kiss a pig.
- Have an "Eat Up Reading" Adventure after hours or a at set time during the school day. This can be a read-a-thon or a shared reading experience with pizza, popcorn, or other snacks donated by local business partners or parent groups.
- Shave the head of a staff member or local celebrity.
- Add a celebration corner in honor of the readers to decorate the school. Post an award certificate that recognizes the success.
- Wear mismatched clothes for a Wacky Wednesday.
- Add a fish tank to the hall or media center.
- Host a storytelling session where students tell their favorite stories or invite a guest storyteller.
- Give a party with cake to celebrate reading.
- Read a special story to a class in an assembly, or over the intercom.
- Plan a special visitor surprise, for example, a favorite author, hero, role model, cartoon character.
- Set a schoolwide time for no homework.
- Hold a special event happening at school. For example, plan a special play day, a musical field day, or a character day.
- Host a VIP (Very Important Person) "Read a Book Day" and invite special visitors to come and read to the classes. Invite parents, community leaders, older students, retired citizens, and local heroes.
- Hold a pep rally with cheers and banners for reading.
- Sponsor a "Books on Parade" or "Character Debut" with students and school personnel dressing up as characters being studied or bringing props of a character.
- Design a T-shirt about a favorite book. Assign a day to wear the special book T-shirt.
- Provide buttons or pencils with a reading slogan.
- Swap teachers for read aloud sessions. Arrange a time periodically to exchange classes for a special reading.
- Have a student or teacher tell about a book or read a selection from a favorite book on the intercom each day or on a special day each week.
- Recognize reading success during morning announcements, in hallway news flashes, or in school newspapers.

Provide a Safe and Accepting Atmosphere

View Errors as Learning Opportunities

Create a learning atmosphere in which the student views his errors as opportunities to improve rather than memorable embarrassing events. Provide options for the student to obtain extra assistance whenever he needs it. Strategically plan a psychologically safe environment that encourages the student to take reading risks with his questions and thinking.

Develop a Team Spirit for Learning

Choose a team name for the class. Remind students that everyone in the class is on the team. Emphasize that the team goal is for everyone to learn as much as possible during the semester or year. Display banners using phrases to promote a reading spirit. Examples:

- Reading makes me a winner.
- Reading takes you to the top.
- Reading trains my brain.

Provide Teaching Opportunities for Students

Provide the students with opportunities to teach each other about the information learned. Organize teaching experiences with individuals or peer groups. Arrange a time for a student to read with other students in other classrooms and grade levels. If time permits, encourage the reader to create a game or activity to accompany the lesson. This gives the student a special avenue to organize, process, and adapt the information read. This time for teaching and reading opportunities is worthwhile because it involves the student in optimal learning experiences. Consider the following example of the impact one teaching experience had on a young student's life.

The mother of a fourth grade student asked a summer school principal to help her daughter, Alex, with reading. The mother said Alex refused to read for pleasure. She had a negative attitude associated with all reading activities.

The principal held brief reading sessions with Alex. They read easy books together. One day Alex read a Dr. Seuss book by herself. The principal suggested that Alex read the book to a kindergarten class and encouraged her to create an activity to use with the book.

After Alex read to the children, she hurried back to the principal's office and said, "Someday I want to be a reading teacher!"

Today Alex is a senior in high school. She started reading with enthusiasm the day she read her book and used the activity she had created with the kindergarten children. Alex's mother reports that she is an honor student who has been an avid reader since that special day when she discovered the joy of reading to the kindergarten children.

THE AFFECTIVE REALMS OF LEARNING

Anything that touches or stirs a feeling influences the reader's emotions and ties directly to his ability to learn. Everything in the students' peripheral vision plays a role in his affective domain. Be aware of how the environment and emotional connections affect the reader.

Rapport and Empathy

A teacher has a tremendous impact on a student's motivation and desire to read. A student will work hard to please the teacher if he likes him. Rapport with the student develops through sharing personal stories, experiences, and common interests. A teacher's excitement in reading about new ideas and facts is contagious. Be a positive role model. Create excitement for learning with observable passion.

Emotions create memorable experiences in learning situations. Design learning activities that stir emotions to create personal connections. For instance, place students "in the author's or character's shoes" so their feelings become an anchor for instruction. Use journaling, character sketches, and reflective activities to record the heights and depths of emotions.

Bibliotherapy heals students' emotional injuries that may be obstacles to learning. For instance, when a student deals with parents' divorce, family separations, marriages, or new siblings, introduce him to books or materials that relate to the event. When the reader sees the situation through the eyes and experiences of others, he develops understanding, empathy, and coping alternatives.

Students know when the teacher genuinely cares. This intuitive feeling makes students know that they are liked and respected. The learners' feeling should be validated and acknowledged with understanding. According to Scheidecker and Freeman (1999), we must construct a new approach to learning—one that accepts and responds to the feelings of the students prior to the dispensation of information. When this occurs, the reader is ready for the assignment. Here are suggestions for strengthening the teacher's bond with students:

- Greet students with a smile.
- Take pictures of the class and display them.
- Write specific "praise" notes to the student.
- Praise the student in front of other students and adults.

- Give the student a "pat on the back" or a high-five for success as he enters and leaves each day.
- Use energizing cheers.
- Plan a picnic, swimming party, or special event for learning celebrations.
- Use humor.
- Praise! Praise! Praise!

Motivation

Motivation is an internal process that guides behavior over time. Being motivated keeps a reader interested and directs his thinking. Teachers need to find each reader's key to internal motivation. Turned-off readers do not learn. The teacher's role in motivating the reader includes the following:

1. *Challenge and stimulate the reader's mind.* Make the reading event interesting and memorable. Build on prior accomplishments and successes. Too many reading experiences in school are boring sessions that turn students off to reading. Students need more challenging reading opportunities that are intriguing and exciting. Too much in school is not interesting to students in today's classroom.

2. *Set up an effective working environment* so that rules are established. Be consistent and persistent. The students make the community of learners and understand "the way we do things around here."

3. *Recognize and reinforce student's successful accomplishments.* Offer helpful, corrective feedback. Ask thought-provoking questions to develop problem solvers and thinkers. Use specific praise for appropriate behaviors and right answers.

4. *Be dynamic! Think out of the box!* Dare to be different so that students never know what stimulating or wacky strategies, activities, or events they will be involved in next.

5. *Adjust assignments to be appropriate for the readers' needs.* Students learn what they want to learn. Accept their unique qualities and strengths. Plan for the diverse needs of readers, so that all master the strategies and skills they need to learn, apply, and succeed. Use a variety of approaches. If the task is too easy, the student may not be motivated. There is a high probability of success when the learning becomes a challenge and the reader is motivated to meet it.

6. *Learn about the students' interests and needs* so that you truly know how to plan for individual needs. Teach at their optimal learning level.

7. *Encourage interaction* among students by setting up a community of learners using brainstorming, partner reading and writing, cooperative learning activities, and role playing.

8. *Provide choices* so students can make decisions about their learning; for example, what they read, where they read, or with whom they read. Accept students' input as to how they can accomplish reading tasks. Invite student involvement.

9. *Create an internal desire to read.* Attitude is altitude! Encourage them to turn their "I cannot do this" to "I can do this!" When readers reach their goals, they are rewarded by their accomplishments. When a reader reaches an obtainable goal, he is motivated by the success of his efforts. Reward effort and improvement.

10. *Be positive and show your passion.* Show you genuinely care. Build a positive relationship with students. Students know when you are sincere and believe they can read and learn.

11. *Create self-directed learners.* If a student feels that the information is meaningful and that he genuinely needs to know it, he will read it.

12. *Realize you make a difference.* Every student needs to be motivated to succeed. Believe in each student. Be the change agent in a reader's life.

Attention, Challenge, Excitement, and Humor

Students spend too many hours reading boring text, completing routine worksheets, or working with activities that are not interesting. There is nothing wrong with texts, worksheets, and assignments if the teacher has made the content come alive, has generated curiosity, and has created excitement in relation to the task. Humor gives a personal connection with the teacher. A good laugh relaxes the brain and prepares it for more information.

Students deserve teachers who care about them and believe they can read. Students deserve teachers who can immerse them in reading material and challenging activities that support and enrich their goals and dreams. Vary your strategies. Make their learning interesting, challenging, and exciting.

Grab the Reader's Attention

Select materials to generate curiosity and interest. Use challenging, fun resources and activities to set a positive classroom tone:

- Jokes, songs, sayings, riddles, cheers, mind twisters, or poems
- Biographies of movie stars, popular singers, music groups, or role models

- Intriguing questions
- Game show formats

Use Anticipation Carrots

Anticipation Carrots lead the student to look forward to upcoming learning encounters. Announce high-interest resources, experiences, or activities before formally presenting them. The following phrases stir curiosity and focus the mind on future learning:

- Read this to discover . . .
- Read this and then you will share what you learned with a classmate.
- You are going to like this.
- When you read this, you are going to find out . . .
- At the end of the unit, we will . . .
- At the end of the week, we will . . .
- Guess what we will do with this information tomorrow!
- Think of ways we can have fun using the information we learned today.

Interweave Interests

Many students are fans of sports heroes, actors and actresses, rock stars, and well-known book characters. Know the student's heroes and special interests, so they can be incorporated as valuable tools to reach the learners in lesson plans and activities. Learn about the individual interests and desires through conversations, conferences, surveys, inventories, and journals. Take the time needed to know your students (Hansen, 2001). Know each learner's interests or hobbies so well that it is easy to carry on a casual conversation with him or her.

Challenge the Mind

Create opportunities for students to work with higher-order thinking skills and mind-challenging activities as they learn new information. Establish an environment where the students yearn to participate and their desire to learn is cultivated daily.

Respect

Choose words and terms to set a positive tone in the classroom. When a student is treated in a kind and respectful way, he learns to return it. Give specific praise of observable behaviors. If possible, avoid negative words and phrases similar to the following:

- Can't
- Don't
- You must
- If you don't
- That's wrong!

Whenever possible, use words and phrases that reflect respect for the student:

- Please.
- Pardon me.
- You'll like this better.
- Be careful when . . .
- Are you comfortable?
- Let me help you . . .
- I like the way you . . .
- You did that well because you . . .

Successful experiences and praise increase students' motivation or desire to read. The teacher's enthusiasm for reading and creating the learning environment has a major impact on the reader's interest. Social interactions while reading with a parent, partner, or small group enhance motivation.

Choice

Intrinsic motivation increases when students are provided with choices in their learning activities (Stipek, 1996). According to Eric Jensen (1995), "Providing choices is the key to motivation." Jensen emphasizes the role of the teacher in finding ways to reach the unmotivated learner. The reader needs opportunities to select his reading material, research methods, activities, presentation strategies, reporting formats, and evaluation tools.

Choice is a motivational tool that builds on the student's interests. It is an effective way to develop confidence, foster independence, and create a sense of responsibility during reading experiences.

Choice Boards

Use a Choice Board that contains mind-challenging activities (see Figure 1.3). This is an effective way to give students voices in their reading. Students enjoy selecting the activities to show what they know, to learn more about the topic, or to apply information in new and different ways. Choice Boards can provide innovative ways for students to show what they have learned from a text passage, a specific reading selection, a unit, or a subject.

Figure 1.3 Choice Board

Design a game based on the subject's facts and trivia.	Write a song that includes the important information.	Create raps, rhymes, or riddles using the vocabulary terms.
Write and illustrate a mini book based on the facts.	Write a front-page news article that includes important facts and details of an event.	Dramatize the procedures, stages, steps, or events in a passage.

The Teacher's Role in Providing Choices

1. Create choice activities based on the reader's needs, ability, and interests.

2. Limit the number of choices, if the reader lacks experiences in making choices. Examples:
   - Use a Four Square outline to design four choices.
   - Use a Tic Tac Toe outline to design nine choices.
   - Use a Bingo Board outline to design twenty-five choices.

3. Provide the reader with opportunities to design activities.

Self-Efficacy

Self-efficacy is an individual's belief in his own ability. Teachers with strong self-efficacy know they use effective classroom management, make learning exciting for students, incorporate the most appropriate resources, and engage parents in positive ways (Bandura, 1997). Self-efficacy is an internal motivator for students, too. If the student believes he cannot read, he is probably not going to be as successful a reader as someone who has confidence in himself.

The Teacher's Role in Building Self-Efficacy

- Teach the reader to praise himself for each reading experience. Examples:

  - I enjoyed reading this passage because. . . .
  - I learned the facts when I read about the topic.
  - I know how to read information on or below my reading level.

- Provide reading models for the reader to imitate. Examples:

  - Listen to recordings of books and poems related to the subject.

- Invite specialists in the subject area to read and share information with the students.
- Give the reader opportunities to read to classmates or students in lower grade levels.
- Set aside a time for the reader to share his successful reading experiences.
- Provide peer to peer rending times with partners or small groups.
- Plan a time to model reading daily.
- Use incentives such as candy and stickers as a last resort.

A COMMUNITY OF READERS

Readers need to feel that they play an important role in the learning culture as members of the team or crew. They know that their diverse strengths and needs are honored. They know that corrected errors move them to new learning. The inviting reading climate fosters on-task behavior, innovative thinking, and active learning that challenges the mind. In the differentiated reading classroom, each reader knows his uniqueness is accepted in the community of learners.

Learn to Read with Me

You see words to read almost everywhere.
In books, TV ads, and on the clothes you wear.

Reading opens new doors to worlds of stuff.
Once you start reading, you can't get enough!

Reading takes you to the deepest part of a great sea
Or to the most remote planets known in our galaxy.

Reading introduces you to people in faraway places.
You hear their lonely cries or see smiles on their faces.

Reading helps you become the person you want to be.
So learn to read wonderful words in our world with me.

—Chapman and King, 2003

Knowing 2
the Reader

Too many students are victims of the unspoken presumption that there is one right way to teach all children to read. But the research on child development and reading styles indicates that what is "appropriate" for one student may be damaging to another.

—Marie Carbo, 1987

The teacher must plan strategically to know each student so that he or she has the opportunity to reach full potential as a reader. When describing diverse learners, the term *diversity* most commonly refers to cultural background, learning styles, and socioeconomic status. But consider the many ways in which readers and learners are diverse:

Gender	Socioeconomic status	Ability
Experiences	Knowledge base	Personality type
Learning styles	Intelligences	Self-concept
Attitude	Physical appearance	Study ethics
Behavior	Learning preferences	Emotions
Values	Fears	Goals and dreams
Language development	Interests	Talents and strengths
Ethnicity	Cultural background	Family support

Begin the quest to know each reader by exploring the reader's background and experiences with language. Strong indicators of skill readiness include writing, speaking, and listening. These skill levels affect the learner's emotions and attitudes toward reading as well as his knowledge base.

How can teachers find time to plan differentiated reading strategies for all students? Time invested in planning the trip and viewing the mission step by step will pay off on the journey. A teacher will do anything to reach a child. It is worth the time to plan for differentiated instruction.

DEVELOPMENTAL READINESS FOR READING

Students approach a concept with their own prior knowledge, so some students will understand a concept and complete a task sooner than others. This base of understanding calls for different paces of instruction to match the needs of the individual learners.

The level of students' independence is developed, allowing more time as needed for experiences and mental processing. Readers who have a broad knowledge base are provided with experiences to extend or enrich their knowledge. Students learn more information, explore areas more purposefully, and are eager to learn when they are learning in their zone of proximal development or level of success.

Differentiated instruction provides an organized, systematic way to meet the needs of all readers. Learning occurs as a gradual, continuous change or in specific stages. In each student, reading skills develop individually over varying periods of time. Learning to read is a building process of exposure, practice, application, and "buy-in." Since every student's journey for reading is unique, teachers must understand individual differences.

The early developmental stages of learning have a major impact on a student's ability and attitudes toward learning to read. For example, a student may blossom as a reader earlier than another child his age. However, a student who learns to read later may become a stronger reader, because he has engaged in activities that developed his small and large motor skills, eye–hand coordination, spatial reasoning, and higher-order thinking skills.

When a preschool child climbs, experiments with musical beats, builds and manipulates objects, role-plays, and communicates, he mentally and physically prepares himself to read. When he explores, discovers, invents, and plays in his creative world, his mental pathways for learning are developing. These early experiences enhance his ability to learn throughout life.

A student may blossom as a reader in the upper grades when he overcomes his reading problems. This occurs when the student's problems are diagnosed correctly and he learns to apply strategies appropriately. An older struggling reader deals with low self-concept, lack of confidence, lack of motivation and weak social relationships. Often, this student is motivated by a teacher or role model who genuinely cares.

MEET YOUR READING CHARACTERS

Most classrooms contain students with characteristics similar to the reading characters described in the following section. Plan strategically to identify each learner's reading behaviors that reflect his unique characteristics and diverse needs. His feelings directly influence his emotions and attitudes toward the reading process. His ability to read can progress and improve with the suggested prescriptions and solutions.

Use the outline that follows with the titles and subheadings as an observation guide to explore each reader's needs, to understand him, and to make assessments. Consider the behavior traits, and add other descriptors. As the student's reading problems are identified, use the outline and suggested prescriptions as a guide to finding solutions.

1. *Reading behaviors:* Identify the reader's specific observable behaviors during reading activities.

2. *Feelings of the student:* Consider the reader's emotions and reactions to reading experiences.

3. *Diagnoses:* Analyze the insights obtained from observations and assessment tools to determine the causes for the reading-related behaviors.

4. *Suggested prescriptions:* Select appropriate solutions to the diagnosed problems using the reader's identified behaviors and feelings. Note that the prescriptions listed here are just a small selection of possible solutions.

EMERGING EMILY

Emerging Emily lacks the skills to become a fluent reader. This student reads below grade level. She struggles with comprehension, phonics, and vocabulary. Sometimes she exhibits inappropriate behaviors. She may keep her feelings hidden. Feelings of defeat have turned off her desire to read. An older student is more likely to hide her inability to read and comprehend. The Emerging Reader at any age deserves the right to be a comprehending reader.

Observations

Reading Behaviors

- Reads very little
- Reads a few words on grade level

- Exhibits poor comprehension skills
- Does not like to read
- Struggles with word attack skills
- Has limited language ability

Feelings of the Student

- I feel lost when I read.
- I will never learn to read, so I will be in this grade the rest of my life.
- I cannot read this assignment.
- I am embarrassed to read, so please do not call on me.
- This is boring and frustrating.
- I will misbehave, so I will not have to read.

Diagnosis and Suggested Prescriptions

Unmotivated

- Pass on the joy and love of reading through modeling it.
- Provide a variety of high-interest, low-level materials.
- Read information aloud or taped as the learner follows the print.
- Create a print-rich environment.
- "Read to" often.

Has a Limited Reading Vocabulary

- Use Language Experience activities.
- Play games with vocabulary words.
- Use repetitive rhymes and short stories.
- Learn basic sight word lists.

Needs Word Attack Skills

- Teach decoding skills.
- Use word families to teach patterns.
- Arrange for someone to read to her often.
- Give the student opportunities to read his own writing.

Lacks the Skills to Bridge Letters to Words,
Words to Sentences, and Sentences to Paragraph

- Reteach, expose, or teach these skills.
- Use letter and word manipulatives.
- Create opportunities to read her own writing.
- Use computer programs and other technology resources.

Lacks Desire to Read Because of Past Failures

- Provide reading choices.
- Create an atmosphere of excitement.
- Implement intriguing pre-reading activities.
- Select guided strategies for the reader's success.
- Allow the student to interpret information using pictures and graphics.
- Give the opportunity to read easy books in her areas of interest.
- Share stories, books, and poems with repetitive rhythms.
- Arrange for this student to read easy books to younger students.

Struggles with the English Language

- Provide stories read in the native language and in English.
- Use picture vocabulary cards with the words written in both languages.
- Label objects in the learner's first language and in English.
- Use actions to demonstrate verbs as they are pronounced.
- Provide a vast amount of oral and written communications in both languages.

WORD-CALLING WAYNE

A Word Caller concentrates on one word at a time, examining the letter sounds before attempting the pronunciation. Listeners become impatient. The reader becomes embarrassed. Word calling hampers comprehension.

Observations

Reading Behaviors

- Reads one or two words at a time
- Lacks oral reading fluency and comprehension
- Does not enjoy reading
- Reacts negatively when asked to read aloud

Feelings of the Student

- I hope no one asks me to read aloud.
- I know I cannot read as well as my friends.
- I understand more when someone reads to me.
- I read it, but I do not know what it says.
- I read it, but I do not know the answers to these questions.
- I am so embarrassed.

Diagnosis with Suggested Prescriptions

Sees One Word at a Time; Eyes Do Not Move Quickly across the Line

- Model reading using short, easy, familiar passages. The student's eyes follow the words.
- Train eyes for left-to-right movement.
- Move a finger or pointer with a continuous rhythm across the lines.
- Move a pen light across the lines.
- Teach skimming and scanning.
- Use choral and echo reading.
- Use assisted reading and gradually remove support.

Overuses Phonics

- Build word recognition speed using repetition of familiar words, phrases. and sentences.
- Use a timer to record and increase reading pace.
- Say the unknown word for the reader to maintain fluency.
- Model sounding out words in the content areas.
- Embed word families in unit lessons.
- Model fluent reading.
- Use games and timed activities to build recognition of basic sight vocabulary words.
- Work on letter–word connection.
- Teach unfamiliar words in isolation before reading.

Works for Perfection

- Teach the value of using various decoding skills to unlock letter sounds.
- Provide opportunities for listening and reading with a model.
- Use partner-reading activities.
- Make stories and books on tape available.
- Consider the reader's insecurity in planning activities.

Lacks Rhythm and Flow While Reading

- Arrange for this student to listen to recorded books and follow the words.
- Read and reread easy books.
- Read with a model reader.
- Record the learner as he reads and listen to the recording.
- Work for perfection on one phrase or sentence before trying another sentence.

Does not follow punctuation symbols

- Teach punctuation meaning and rules.
- Emphasize punctuation with an action for each symbol. Example: Finger snap = period
- Demonstrate and practice use of each punctuation with color-coding. Example: red = period
- Use a sound for each punctuation symbol. Example: a "pop" sound made with the lips = period

Needs Confidence

- Make available recorded books and stories.
- Provide easy reading materials.
- Practice reading repetitive phrases and rhymes.
- Arrange for the student to listen to stories.
- Provide reading from language experience.
- Plan time for the student to read to younger children.

Has a Low Mastered Vocabulary

- Teach words used every day.
- Play games with vocabulary words.
- Provide a print-rich environment at school and home.
- Encourage other teachers and tutors to carry on conversations related to the content lessons and experiences.
- Use read-along strategies.

INSECURE INEZ

An Insecure Reader does not want to make mistakes in the presence of others. Her low self-esteem is evident. She does not have a sense of belonging. An inadequate knowledge base in one subject may be the source of this insecurity; the insecurity may not be evident in another subject.

Observations

Reading Behaviors

- Uncomfortable with reading capabilities
- Afraid of mistakes and failure
- Slow to let others know how and what she knows
- Does not feel successful as a reader

Feelings of the Student

- I don't want to be wrong.
- I hope no one laughs at me.
- I do not believe I can do this.
- I don't want to disappoint my teacher, my parents, or myself.
- If I read slowly, I will not make as many mistakes.
- I have never understood my science books.

Diagnosis and Suggested Prescriptions

Afraid to Show What She Knows

- Use authentic assessment tools other than total class questioning.
- Build confidence with easy reading materials.
- Ask questions you know she can answer.
- Find her "best" way to read and comprehend.

Feels Peer Pressure

- Provide opportunities for success.
- Work with small group instruction.
- Allow her to choose a partner.
- Provide individual instruction.

Shy and Nervous

- Allow longer wait time for responses.
- Praise successes.
- Use Choice Boards so the student selects activities in her comfort zone.
- Provide opportunities for the reader to respond privately to questions.
- Make short assignments that give her success.
- Let her choose a respected or admired reading partner.
- Use one-on-one instructional strategies.

Experienced Too Many
Failures and Negative Feedback

- Probe with effective questions.
- Use the learner's knowledge base to develop instructional plans.
- Provide confidence-building opportunities.
- Give specific praise and positive reinforcement.
- Turn the "I can't" attitude into "I can" feelings.

Has Created Emotional Barriers to Learning

- Provide easy, enjoyable reading materials.
- Give choices.
- Provide high-interest reading resources.
- Showcase the student's talents.
- Brag on the student's strengths and successes.
- Provide opportunities for her to share her knowledge of topics of interest.

TURNED-OFF TOM

The Turned-off Reader is capable of reading and comprehending, but he is unchallenged and unmotivated. He needs a strong "buy-in" or interest in the reading activity or assignment.

Observations

Reading Behaviors

- Exhibits a negative attitude with most reading assignments
- Refuses to complete reading activities and assignments
- Doesn't see a purpose for reading
- Reflects his "don't care" attitude through body language and demeanor

Feelings of the Student

- I do not need to read this.
- I don't like to read about . . .
- I wish these teachers would "get with it" and find something I want to read.
- Why would anyone want to waste time reading this boring information?

Diagnosis with Suggested Prescriptions

Needs Positive Experiences in All
Reading Activities and Assignments

- Provide a non-threatening environment with a comfortable spot to read.
- Model reading.
- Conduct conferences to give the student opportunities to verbalize his feelings about reading.
- Use immediate, specific, positive feedback.

Needs Choices Around Interests

- Provide high-interest books and materials.
- Select a wide variety of reading materials on various reading levels.
- Provide choices in reading topics and genres.
- Use a survey to match books to the reader's interest areas.
- Ask the reader to choose books for the classroom library.

Needs to See a
Significance in the Reading Activity

- Create effective pre-reading experiences.
- Present each assignment with a meaningful purpose that illustrates the student's need to read the information.
- Provide meaningful, interesting follow-up activities based on the reading passage.
- Assign short passages.

CORRECTING CARL

The Correcting Reader blurts out the correct pronunciation of a word or the answer to a question. Often, he is unconscious of his disruptive, inappropriate behavior. He enjoys adding his comments to the information. The reading pace is too slow for him. He volunteers the corrections to speed the reading process along. It is easy to squelch his reading enthusiasm.

Observations

Reading Behaviors

- Blurts out inappropriately
- Answers out of turn
- Lacks respect for others
- Needs and yearns to be heard
- Thinks best when thinking aloud

Feelings of the Student

- I know this word, so I will show my friends how smart I am.
- When I say a word aloud, I understand it.
- When I know the answers, everyone needs to hear me.

Diagnosis and Suggested Prescriptions

Wants to Be Heard

- Make student aware of expectations for listening.
- Have a private conference to discuss the rules for taking turns.
- Explain the need for other students to have a turn.
- Provide opportunities for the student to assist a reader through small group or partner activities.

Eager to Move On, So Answers for Classmates

- Establish rules for taking turns.
- Teach appropriate listening tools.
- Teach him to respect other students and adults.
- Establish a self-monitoring system.

Has Nervous Energy

- Provide prompts and signals as reminders.
- Reward correct behavior with specific praise.
- Provide challenging opportunities and activities.
- Arrange for the student to be actively engaged.

READ ALOUD RENEE

The Read Aloud Reader comprehends. She has to hear the words. Read Aloud Renee is an auditory learner. She is an excellent oral reading volunteer because she reads enthusiastically and comprehends. During silent reading, she often has difficulty understanding the information.

Observations

Reading Behaviors

- Is a fluent, oral, comprehending reader
- Has a strong sight vocabulary
- Volunteers to read orally
- Reads orally with confidence, enthusiasm, and expression
- Answers comprehension questions accurately after reading aloud
- Understands what she reads when reading orally

Feelings of the Student

- I like to read to others.
- I wish I could read with a partner.

- I do not like to read silently.
- Sometimes I wish I could move on instead of spending so much time reading and discussing a passage.

Diagnosis with Suggested Prescriptions

Maintains a Strong Reading Vocabulary

- Reinforce and add to her vocabulary knowledge base.
- Provide materials that challenge in her range of success.

Possesses a Reading Passion

- Provide opportunities to read aloud for varying purposes.
- Use a variety of reading materials on high-interest, challenging levels.

Has Mastered Oral Reading Skills

- Permit the student to share her personal fulfillment and success from reading.
- Nurture the talent! Be careful not to take advantage of it.
- Provide special reading privileges in read aloud sessions.

Has Difficulty Reading Silently

- Play silent comprehension games.
- Use brief passages for silent reading assignments.
- Provide a private space for reading chosen by the reader, if possible.
- Accept the student's need to lip read and mumble.
- Allow the student to read into an elbow-shaped pipe. Hold the pipe in the position of a telephone receiver so she can hear herself read.

SILENT READING SAM

A Silent Reader comprehends when he reads to himself. When he reads orally or someone reads to him, he does not comprehend as well. This student is strong academically and an effective reader throughout his lifetime because most reading is done independently. As an older student, he does not volunteer to read aloud unless he has had time to practice reading the selection.

Observations

Reading Behaviors

- Comprehends while reading silently
- Has a strong sight reading vocabulary

- Uses context clues
- Enjoys reading silently
- Does not comprehend as well when read to or when he reads aloud
- Is more productive when assigned silent reading

Feelings of the Student

- I don't want my friends to hear me read.
- I know what the author is saying when I read to myself.
- No one will be able to correct my reading and embarrass me, if I read alone.
- I can read this book at my own pace in my own way.
- I need to read this information to myself.
- I do not like to read aloud.
- I hope I am not called on to read aloud.

Diagnosis with Suggested Prescriptions

Strong, Independent Silent Reader

- Provide time for this student to read independently.
- Provide time to read the assigned passage silently, before reading it aloud.
- Give him opportunities to choose his reading materials to read silently.
- Call on him to answer comprehension questions after silent reading.

Weak in Auditory Skills

- Make arrangements to read with a stronger reader.
- Allow student to read along with a tape or a CD.
- Use shared reading activities.
- Use oral rhythmic pattern reading.

Views Oral Reading as a Time Waster

- Provide partner and small group read aloud activities with short segments.
- Give positive feedback through praise for oral reading.
- Explain the purposes of oral reading.

COMPREHENDING CARLOS

A Comprehending Learner understands the reading passages during silent and oral reading. He is a fluent reader who enjoys most reading experiences.

Observations

Reading Behaviors

- Comprehends as an oral or silent reader
- Enjoys reading
- Understands, interprets, and adapts information before, during, and after reading a selection
- Has strong word attack skills and a large sight vocabulary
- Prepared developmentally to grasp the reading process

Feelings of the Student

- I like to read.
- I know what the author is telling me.
- I do not always understand why others struggle with reading.
- I wish I could read what I want to read.
- I wish I could answer these questions without waiting on everyone.

Diagnosis and Suggested Prescriptions

Needs Challenge with High-Interest Materials

- Provide reading choices.
- Make a wide variety of reading materials available.
- Assign readings in various genres.
- Provide opportunities for him to share his enthusiasm as a fluent reader with others.

Needs Higher-Order Thinking Activities

- Assign reading-related projects and assignments to build problem-solving skills.
- Provide research opportunities to extend his knowledge base.
- Ask mind-provoking questions before, during, and after reading.

DEVELOPING THE EAGER, FLUENT READER

There is no magic formula for developing an eager, fluent reader. We know from extensive research and effective practices that certain elements create a learning community for the successful reader. These elements include the following:

Diagnosis and Assessment

1. Know the individual student's needs.

2. Learn how to use various reading assessment and diagnostic tools.

3. Know how to match the diagnosis and assessment tools to the reader's needs.

4. Explore the characteristics and behaviors of the individual reader.

5. Identify specific reading problems and apply corrective procedures.

Instruction

1. Plan differentiated instruction to reach the individual's needs.

2. Infuse reading comprehension, word attack skills, and vocabulary strategies into daily instruction.

3. Expose the learner to enthusiastic, stimulating, expressive reading models.

4. Scaffold instruction by introducing new skills within reach of the reader's success.

5. Use meaningful activities to develop understanding before, during, and after each reading assignment.

6. Use flexible grouping.

7. Teach to reach the student in the many ways he learns.

8. Vary formats by reading to and with the student. Strategically plan time for silent and oral reading.

9. Create intriguing experiences for the student to understand, use, and appreciate various genres.

Tools and Strategies

1. Model each strategy in a purposeful manner.

2. Teach the student how to select, personalize, and apply reading strategies.

3. Show the student how to create and use mnemonic devices to memorize, use, adapt, and retain information for long-term use.

4. Use a variety of strategies to teach a skill or concept.

5. Immerse the learner in challenging, high-interest reading materials on his ability level.

Materials

1. Provide a wide variety of materials and resources based on the student's interests and needs.

2. Select novel materials on the reader's level of understanding.

3. Provide meaningful purposes for personal experiences with text-related materials.

Environment

1. Know the student's interests.

2. Provide reading experiences that relate to the student's life.

3. Keep the reader actively involved.

4. Spark the learner's desire to read.

5. Set high expectations with the daily belief that he is a reader.

6. Provide the least restrictive environment.

7. Establish a challenging learning climate.

8. Accept and honor individual diversity.

9. Exude enthusiasm as a reading model.

THE KEYS TO READING SUCCESS

Observe the student and assess each unique situation. Assess the student before, during, and after reading. Chart the information. Look for behaviors of students. Diagnose and prescribe. Remember, each student can learn to read. You hold the key to the reader's success.

Reading Problems and Solutions

Solutions to reading problems begin with the teacher. A student does not know how to eliminate or overcome his problem. When a student has a reading difficulty, it hinders his ability to comprehend subject information. He is usually embarrassed when asked to read. Often this learner develops a "don't care" attitude. This struggling reader needs solutions to his problems.

Effective teachers keep students actively involved and engaged. They know that to learn something well you also have to teach it. So they model solutions and then let the students practice them. They give the students positive reinforcement for getting answers right, making discoveries, and exploring the world adventures. Effective teachers use coaching and

Figure 2.1   Reading problems and solutions

Observable Characteristics	Possible Problems	Suggested Solutions
Reads one word at a time	• Insecurity • Visual perception • Too much focus on decoding • May be reading from right to left and then left to right	• Assign shorter passages • Give pen light as pointer • Check eyesight • Give a marker, such as a pointer Allow to use finger to follow the lines
Words move on the page while trying to read	• Visual problem	• Use colored transparency overlays • Have sunglasses available with different colored lenses (yellow, green, rose, blue). See if reads better with color.
Incorrect posture	• Lack interest in assignment • Insecurity • Appears to be a lazy reader	• Model appropriate posture • Provide chaise reading spots
Easily distracted	• Does not complete tasks • Used to working alone	• Needs quiet place to read • Needs directions given one step at a time • Give specific praise for concentrating and staying on task
Complains that the room is too quiet during independent reading	• Cannot concentrate on what he is reading in a quiet environment	• Play background music • Use personal music and headphones • Ask specific questions from text to see that music is improving concentration
Lips move while reading	• Developed this as a habit! • Often an auditory learner • Slows down the reading • Sometimes a Word Caller • Hinders comprehension	• Strategy used to focus and concentrate, so sometimes needs to lip read • Teach to move faster across the lines for comprehension
Trouble keeping place	• Easily distracted • Usually not interested in reading	• Needs a marker, pointer, or finger to follow the words and stay on the right line • Use fewer words on the page • Needs shorter assignments
Reads, but does not know what he has read	• Is not comprehending • Has not learned to focus • Does not follow directions well	• Use personal stories from the student's writing portfolio to get him to read and then rephrase • Teach and model comprehension strategies • Find out if the reader can comprehend if someone reads the passage aloud to him

modeling and then turn the practice over to the students. Teachers who honor diversity continually assess, model, coach, and guide practice when planning effective instruction.

Multiple Intelligences in the Reading Classroom

Effective teachers plan learning experiences that nurture and enhance student intelligences across a wide range of learning styles, including multiple intelligences (Gardner, 1983), thinking as a reader (Sternberg, 1996), cognitive learning styles (Gregorc, 1985), and 4Mat theory (McCarthy, 1997). (See Figures 2.2–2.6.)

Figure 2.7 offers a metaphor that students can use to compare their learning preferences to such objects as a clipboard, microscope, puppy, or beach ball. Demystifying and becoming aware of their own characteristics will help students to understand why they do the things they do in the classroom. Activity:

- Ask students to identify which of those objects most closely symbolizes their preferences.
- Have students rank the object preferences from 1 (most like them) to 4 (least like them).
- Ask the students to write or tell why they made their top two choices.
- By knowing the activities that represent their learning preferences, students will feel more encouraged to work within their favorite comfort zones.

The Role of Pleasure in Reading Practice

A struggling reader seldom experiences pleasure when reading. He loses the flow of thought during his efforts to pronounce and understand the meaning of individual words and phrases. Usually he is embarrassed to read aloud, but he also realizes that reading silently is useless because he cannot comprehend the information and respond to questions.

A learner may read well but lack motivation because he prefers to be entertained. He does not find the topics appealing or interesting to read. If a student is interested in the subject, he will read it. For example, most students respond to reading experiences related to videos, movies, computers, music, heroes, and clothing styles.

Keep in mind that each student varies in his stages of developmental growth, so his interests and needs constantly change (see Figures 2.8 and 2.9). The effective teacher conducts surveys, inventories, and personal conversations with students to identify and use the students' talents and interests in planning lessons.

(Text continues on page 52)

Figure 2.2 Multiple intelligences in the reading classroom

Verbal/Linguistic	Musical/Rhythmic	Visual/Spatial	Logical/Mathematical
• Is a fluent reader • Listens attentively • Communicates in writing • Links new and prior learning • Debates issues • Researches topics • Expresses a point of view • Reads for pleasure • Enjoys listening to someone read • Uses verbal mnemonics • Chunks information • Uses language to communicate effectively	• Comprehends with background music playing while reading • Finds interest stimulated with beats • Looks for rhythmic patterns and poetry • Spells words to a beat • Attacks words by dividing them into syllables • Creates songs, poems, jingles, or raps to remember information • Enjoys reading while playing background music that depicts the setting • Relates to the sound of a setting	• Color-codes and highlights • Doodles while listening • Visualizes pictures while reading about events, character descriptions, and settings • Uses graphic organizers to plot thinking • Needs visual hooks • Views, interprets, or draws pictures and graphics to understand text • Prepares visuals or PowerPoint presentations • Uses art to express understanding	• Organizes information • Outlines and classifies data • Yearns to understand sequence of the information • Learns by using timelines and step-by-step procedures • Reasons logically • Needs clear, precise directions • Learns trivia facts • Enjoys logic-related games and puzzles • Thinks abstractly and critically • Uses the computer and other gadgets • Is a problem solver

(Continued)

Figure 2.2 Continued

Bodily/Kinesthetic	Naturalist	Intrapersonal	Interpersonal
• Learns by role-playing • Simulates events • Creates artifacts • Needs centers, labs, and hands-on learning opportunities • Needs a comfortable spot of choice to read and work • Can skillfully use the body • Uses manipulatives to explore, learn, and discover • Can show it or demonstrate it • Needs to move to learn • Responds to actions and feelings of characters	• Yearns to discover with nature • Intuitively relates and learns factual information about science and the world around him • Creates habitats • Conducts experiments • Is a survivor • Sees patterns in nature • Copes and survives in most environments • Relates to events and settings	• Works best independently • Needs time to make personal application • Reflects in a journal • Is self-reflective • Needs time to process new learning independently • Needs a quiet space to read and work • Accepts goals and responsibilities • Enjoys reading alone • Learns with personal links and connections	• Works best with others • Enjoys partner reading • Communicates with others • Learns through interactions such as text or literary talks • Empathizes with struggling readers • Needs to talk while learning • Works well in flexible groupings • Enjoys discussions • Is a social butterfly • Understands others' feelings and emotions • Needs interaction, conversations, and discussions. • Needs a listening ear

Figure 2.3 Comprehension tasks for students

Verbal/ Linguistic	Musical/Rhythmic	Logical/Mathematical	Visual/Spatial
• Write a summary. • Make a prediction. • Discuss the relationships. • Vary genres. • Debate issues. • Take notes. • Write reflectively. • Write creatively. • Make a class presentation.	• Write a song to describe. • Create a musical game. • Make a CD, video, or tape. • Find background music. • Create the sounds of the setting. • Create a song, rap, poem, cheer or jingle. • Create a rhythmic pattern.	• Create a timeline. • Conduct a comparison. • Compare/contrast. • Develop a graph using data. • Write the sequence. • Develop a training guide. • Conduct an experiment. • Use a game show format. • Create a calendar of events • Develop a sequence. • Use a matrix. • Use the computer.	• Make a collage. • Videotape a scene. • Create a poster. • Paint a mural. • Invent a board game. • Sketch or draw. • Sequence scenes. • Draw a cartoon. • Plot on a graphic organizer.

Bodily/Kinesthetic	Naturalist	Intrapersonal	Interpersonal
• Role-play. • Take on the role of a character. • Create flannel board stories. • Build a model. • Create an adventure game. • Create a display. • Conduct experiments. • Investigate and explore.	• Relate information to nature. • Understand relationships. • Categorize. • Form a hypothesis. • Label and classify. • Predict. • Draw conclusions.	• Reflect. • Read independently. • Research. • Study the information. • Take notes. • Do a project. • Question. • Use self-talk.	• Read and work with a partner. • Work with a small group. • Use cooperative learning. • Use choral reading. • Conduct a service project. • Join a conversation circle. • Do a group project. • Interview. • Give the character's point of view. • Have a mock trial.

Adapted from Chapman C., & King, R. *Test Success in the Brain Compatible Classroom. Tucson, AZ: Zephyr Press. 2000.*

Figure 2.4 Sternberg's thinking as a reader

Practical	Analytical	Creative
• How can I use this information? • The author said this in order to show _____. • Think of a time when you _____.	• What are the facts? • The steps to this procedure are _____. • What does this say? • Compare the facts.	• Think of other ways. • Why do you think this happened? • Predict what will happen next. • How will I share what I have learned? • How can I apply this? • How can I use this information in a new way?

Figure 2.5 Gregorc's learning styles

Concrete/Sequential	Abstract/Sequential
➤ Desires to learn ➤ Uses lists, timelines, procedural directions to create order ➤ Seeks details to support ideas ➤ Needs hands-on activities with manipulatives and experiments ➤ Thrives on personal engagement in reading-related experiences	➤ Yearns for order and procedure ➤ Applies analytical thinking ➤ Uses visual imagery ➤ Adapts rational and logical thinking while reading ➤ Wants to investigate and analyze ➤ Needs time to process information read ➤ Seeks personal connections to reading
Concrete/Random	**Abstract/Random**
➤ Is a divergent thinker ➤ Enjoys finding alternative ways to complete reading tasks ➤ Thrives on reading choices ➤ Understands the "big picture" quickly ➤ Learns through trial and error	➤ Is flexible and spontaneous ➤ Reads best with a partner or group ➤ Feelings and emotions are interwoven though each reading activity ➤ Needs a non-threatening environment ➤ Seeks variety ➤ Discovers the answer but may not know how or why

Figure 2.6   4Mat models

Type I: The Imaginative Reader (Asks "Why?")	Type II: The Analytical Reader (Asks "What?")
• Uses feelings and reflections • Asks questions • Makes predictions and asks "What if . . . ?" • Discusses ideas • Asks "Why?" while reading • Questions content and reading purposes • Seeks to understand author and character motives • Needs to make personal connections to reading • Brainstorms effectively • Seeks alternative solutions	• Seeks facts • Organizes information • Analyzes and categorizes • Works systematically • Needs strong pre-reading lead-ins • Learns with advanced organizers • Needs clear, specific purposes, directions, and expectations • Needs to receive interesting materials to be motivated to read • Make judgments quickly • Uses charts, graphs, lists, and graphic organizers • Reflects and then acts
Type III: The Common Sense Reader (Asks "How?")	Type IV: The Dynamic Reader (Asks "What can this become?")
• Seeks usability • Wants practical applications • Prefers to learn by trying things out • Needs to be encouraged to experiment • Asks "How can I apply this in my world?" • Prefers reality • Readily compares and contrasts	• Needs permission to create • Enjoys freedom to risk with thinking • Thinks out of the box • Has an innate desire to work independently, but works well in groups, too • Believes in his own influence • Avoids routine • Enjoys activities related to personal growth and renewal

Adapted from McCarthy, 1990

Figure 2.7 The object and you

Clipboard	Microscope
• Needs set procedures • Works with clear, precise directions • Seeks structure • Learns with guided reading instruction • Is productive in Language Experience	• Investigates and discovers • Asks "Why?" • Needs experiments • Focuses on the supporting details • Enjoys research • Digs for evidence • Analyzes
Puppy	Beach ball
• Needs comfortable spot to read • Is productive during group work • Likes peer-to-peer tutoring • Wants consensus • Needs a safe climate • Has a strong need to belong • Wants everyone to be happy	• Needs a variety of reading materials • Likes choices and flexibility • Enjoys brainstorming • Yearns for movement • Enjoys using variation • Engages in active learning and participation • Seeks fun and excitement • Uses effective hooks to focus • Requires novelty

Common Needs of All Learners

All learners need challenging environments in which they learn varied strategies to retain information they need and want to know. They deserve respect for their backgrounds, experiences, risk-taking ideas, and diverse abilities. All learners need time to think, process, and apply information as they develop a new knowledge base. Specific approval provides internal feedback. Include positive reading models who provide opportunities for them to fulfill their visions, goals, and dreams in emotionally safe havens.

ASSESSING AND DIAGNOSING THE READER

Assessment provides a clear, concrete way to determine what the student needs to learn. The assessment process is ongoing. The student and the teacher monitor progress. The information determines future learning opportunities. Use the results of your checklists and surveys to plan differentiated lessons and grouping designs. Portfolios provide important assessment data to guide conferences with the student, parent, or student support team.

Figure 2.8 Developmental characteristics of students in lower grades

	Agree	Disagree	Comments
Filled with curiosity and wonder for learning			
Lives in a "me" world			
Excited about learning			
Wants to make the world a better place			
Exhibits emotional highs and lows			
Devastates emotionally in defeat for a brief time			
Needs support in all stages of learning			
Influenced by adults and friends			
Needs hands-on activities to process information related to skills			
Takes risks			
Explores orally			
Must have a variety of experiences to build a knowledge base			
Sees the world through rose-colored glasses			
Needs to play, explore, create, discover, and invent.			
Develops small/large motor skills			
Has untapped potential			
Needs positive role models			
Thrives with people who care about them			
Aims to please			
Other			

Figure 2.9 Developmental characteristics of students in the upper grades

	Agree	Disagree	Comments
Thinks about "self"			
Prefers unhealthy foods			
Desires approval			
Is sensitive			
Exhibits highs and lows			
Varies in maturity level			
Yearns to do things "his way"			
Is influenced by role models			
Needs outlets for energy			
Is self-conscious			
Personalizes problems			
Needs peer approval			
Desires recognition			
Seeks adult guidance other than parents			
Is led easily by "heroes"			
Needs real-life activities			
Others			

Remember, the best surveys, checklists, and rubrics are designed by teachers. Because teachers know the students, they recognize the traits, concepts, standards, or skills they need to assess.

Checklists are easy to use in daily observations. Use the following checklist to assess the status of the reader. You can use this guide periodically throughout the year to watch the reader grow and record your observations on the grid (Figure 2.10). Some characteristics may be checked in each section.

Figure 2.10 Observation grid for reader status checklist

Observation 1	Observation 2	Observation 3
Date _____	Date _____	Date _____
_____ Emerging	_____ Emerging	_____ Emerging
_____ Successful	_____ Successful	_____ Successful
_____ Fluent	_____ Fluent	_____ Fluent
Comments	Comments	Comments
Observer _____	Observer _____	Observer _____

Reader Status Checklist

Student _____   Class _____

Check all that apply.

Emerging Reader

_____ Understands eye movement directions: left to right and top to
bottom

_____ Uses picture clues

_____ Knows initial and final consonant sounds

_____ Knows the difference in letters and words

_____ Demonstrates limited sight word vocabulary

_____ Responds to some punctuation signs

_____ Exhibits behaviors that reflect insecurity and feelings of
hopelessness

_____ Demonstrates inadequate comprehension skills

_____ Shows limited ability to decode unfamiliar words

_____ Displays attitudes toward reading during reading activities

Successful Reader

_____ Actively uses background knowledge as links to new
information

_____ Is a confident reader

_____ Applies decoding skill

_____ Interprets text information on grade level

_____ Uses self-corrective reading strategies

_____ Engages in meaningful thinking while reading

_____ Remembers facts and general concepts

Fluent Reader

_____ Is an avid reader

_____ Uses context clues

_____ Has a broad sight vocabulary

_____ Makes self-corrections

_____ Decodes automatically

_____ Uses information in higher-order thinking

_____ Interprets purposes and meanings of reading activities

_____ Enjoys reading in various genres

Surveys and Inventories

Learn as much about the students as possible. Effective assessments are ongoing and differentiated to meet the needs and the purposes of the learning. To personalize the reading culture, develop surveys, inventories, checklists, and rubrics to identify the students' needs in specific situations.

Surveys are valuable tools that assist teachers in getting to know the students' attitudes toward reading. Tune in to the student's thoughts, beliefs, interests, fears, and dreams. Use the surveys to personalize instruction and develop meaningful connections between the learner's life and the subject information. The following surveys may be adapted to all grade levels to survey student beliefs, interests, and environmental factors relevant to reading and learning:

Sample Interest Survey

1. My favorite way to spend time is _____
   _____.

2. I earn money by _____
   _____.

3. I do not like to _____
   _____.

4. My favorite television show is _____
   _____.

5. My favorite movie is _____
   _____.

6. My favorite subject is _____
   _____.

7. The most difficult thing I do at school is _____
   _____.

8. The easiest thing I do at school is _____
   _____.

9. The reading materials I have at home are _____
   _____.

10. I spend the following number of hours a week doing each of these:
   ___ Watching television   ___ Listening to the radio
   ___ Talking on the telephone   ___ Working on homework
   ___ Playing a sport   ___ Spending time with friends
   ___ Other

11. The following people read to me: _____
   _____.

12. Currently I am reading _____
   _____.

13. I like to read when _____
   _____.

14. My favorite author is _____
   _____.

15. I enjoy reading about _____
   _____.

16. I enjoy listening to stories about _____
   _____.

Student Beliefs Survey

Give the student opportunities to answer questions that uncover his core values and beliefs:

1. If you had a million dollars, how would you spend it?

2. Name five things you would like to do now or later in your life.

3. How do you like to spend your free time?

4. What are your hobbies and interests?

5. What do you read?

6. What do you do after school?

7. What is the first thing you think when someone asks you to read aloud?

8. How do you feel when you have a reading assignment to complete alone?

9. What are two of the best books you have heard or read?

10. What is the worst experience you have had with reading?

11. What are two of the best experiences you have had with reading?

Figure 2.11 Where am I as a learner?

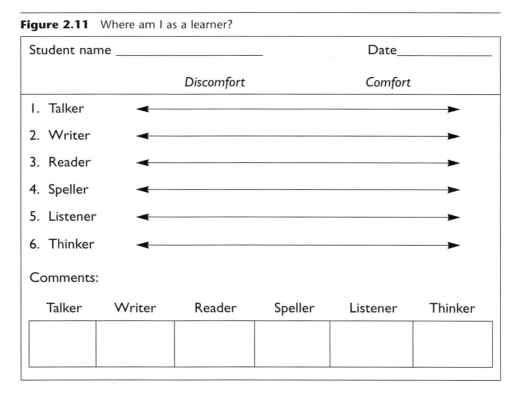

Use the following scale in a conference with the student reader. Analyze and discuss the responses with the reader. Explain the terms "comfort" and "discomfort." Ask the reader to place an X on each line to indicate his comfort level in each area.

Figure 2.12 Student interest survey

Student name _____   Date_____

1. Place a plus sign (+) beside three things you like to do most after school.
2. Put a minus sign (−) beside three things that are your least favorite things to do after school.
3. Add other areas as needed.

	Work on a computer	Play games outside
	Talk on the phone	Go to a movie
	Watch television	Practice for a game with my team
	Read a book	Take dance lessons
	Work for pay	Take special classes
	Visit with my friends	Spend time with my parents
	Other	Other

Describe your favorite hobbies, pastimes, or interests.

1	2	3

Give reasons for choosing each of your least favorite ways to spend time.

1	2	3

Poll students with a survey to identify their interests. Their responses provide a foundation for planning lessons and building rapport with them. Here is a sample.

Home Environment Survey

1. Do you have a specific time to study at home?

2. Do you have a room of your own?

3. Do you have access to a computer?

4. How much time do you spend watching TV each day?

5. How much time do you spend on computers?

6. Do your parents keep track of your work activities at school?

7. What kind of reading materials are in your home?

SUMMARY

Each reader's knowledge base, learning styles, intelligences, and attitude play a major role in his success with each reading activity. When the teacher identifies the learner's background knowledge and the many ways he learns, it is easier to plan activities to meet his unique needs as a reader.

Design each lesson to give the reader successful experiences as he learns. Before the pace of instruction is set, consider the individual reader's developmental readiness for the specific skill. If a skill is too difficult, the reader will be frustrated. If the skill is too easy, the reader will be bored. The challenge is to orchestrate each lesson so the skill is within the reader's level of success.

Each reader's diverse needs become evident through his behaviors in daily activities. His emotions and reactions during reading experiences indicate his feelings related to reading. Always remember that past experiences usually determine the reader's negative or positive response to reading activities. Keep a log of observable behaviors and use the information as an integral part of the reader's assessment.

Use a variety of assessment tools to gather information. Use the data to diagnose the reader's problems and prescribe solutions. Use the reader's strengths to strengthen his weaknesses, for example, if he has difficulty comprehending the text and he excels with art, encourage him to use visual imagery to illustrate the information. Also use the reader's strengths to expand his strongest abilities, for example, if the reader is a fluent, comprehending reader, encourage him to investigate related topics and share information in a presentation or special exhibit.

Know the characteristics of the reading characters in your classroom. Use this knowledge to create a reading environment that builds on interests, generates excitement, supports effort, encourages, and inspires each reader.

Models of **3** Reading

The models of reading discussed in this chapter provide a structure for classroom instruction. The student needs to see each strategy modeled. He needs to practice the procedures in the model with the teacher's guidance.

Each model is designed for immediate use in the classroom within the content area curriculum. Adapt the suggestions and guidelines to your teaching strategies. Choose the reading model that matches your students' needs to enhance their reading skills.

ADJUSTABLE ASSIGNMENTS MODEL

Adjustable Assignments are used to plan for the teaching of one topic, standard, skill, objective, or essential question. When a teacher works through the planning of an Adjustable Assignment, students benefit (see Figure 3.1) (Gregory & Chapman, 2002a).

With Adjustable Assignments, the learner begins with what he knows and then moves into what he needs to know. If the teacher analyzes the needs of a group of students, he can plan strategically for that group of students. Learners are able to work through activities and tasks that meet their particular needs.

An appropriate pre-assessment tool is administered to find out what the students know. The information learned from the assessment is the student's knowledge base. If a teacher knows specific information about a reader's background knowledge on a topic, he can plan the appropriate actions to take to help the reader grow in his learning.

Figure 3.1   Adjustable Assignment model

Standard _____

Pre-assessment Tool _____

C		How will I teach each group?	
B	What skill does each group need to	learn next?	
A	What does each group know about	this topic?	
	High Degree of Mastery	Approaching Mastery	Beginning

Adapted from Gregory and Chapman, 2002a

CURRICULUM COMPACTING MODEL

To meet the needs of high-end learners in a particular topic, Joe Renzulli of the University of Connecticut (Renzulli et al., 2000; see also Tomlinson, 1999, 2001) designed the Curriculum Compacting model.

Many readers study and explore the world as researchers and di coverers of information. If a student is an expert on a topic or has mastered a standard or skill, he needs a special plan so he can grow in his knowledge. This student deserves an alternative assignment. See Figure 3.2 for an adjustable model that shows levels of readiness for research assignments.

CENTERS AND PROJECTS MODEL

Add projects, labs, centers, cooperative groups, and personalized instruction to your classroom. Design periods of time for hands-on experiences to make learning happen. Independent and small groups work at manipulative stations experiencing content in meaningful ways. This allows students to take control of their learning.

Centers or Work Stations

Stations are set up as an assembly-line process where students work in each center. The activities can be leveled according to difficulty. Centers may be assigned to meet a student's needs. Examples of hands-on centers include:

Figure 3.2 Adjustable model for research

• Has resources and uses effectively • Topic clearly defined and expanded • Works independently and productively • Reflects creativity • Accurate information	• Uses two or more sources to locate information • Stays on topic • Little assistance needed • Some awareness of purpose • Some organization shown	• Uses one source for given topic • Lapse in unity of topic • Ongoing assistance required • Poor awareness of purpose • Poor organization of thoughts
High Degree of Mastery	Approaching Mastery	Beginning

Adapted from Gregory and Chapman, 2002a

Often a student is gifted or expert in a specific area or topic. Joe Renzulli of the University of Connecticut (see also Tomlinson, 1999, 2001) designed the Curriculum Compacting Model to meet the needs of this high-end learner. A student may already know about the subject because he studied and explored it as a researcher and discoverer of information. When a reader has mastered a standard or skill, he needs a special plan so he can continue to grow in his knowledge. This learner deserves alternative assignments.

PROJECT – BASED MODELS

Project-based learning fosters in-depth studies about a topic. Everyone is given the same assignment, guidelines, rubric, and timeline, but the products vary. For example, students may all receive an assignment to create a travel brochure with the same criteria and grading rubric, but every brochure will have a different appearance because different destinations are depicted. Students may use any media to present their brochures.

In a *Multiple Intelligences Model,* lists of the possible project assignments are created around the targeted intelligences, with students choosing the project they prefer.

In a *Student Choice Contract Model,* the student presents a proposal to the teacher for a project. This would include the student's idea, reasons, procedure, and product. It would have to be approved by the teacher. Guidelines, criteria, and rubrics are set by the teacher, so that standards and expectations for the project are established.

Project Content Questions

- Will the project be an ongoing part of the instruction in one or more of the content areas?
- Will the project be a culminating activity to show what the student has learned within a specific area of focus or topic?
- Will the project be a shared home and school commitment?
- Will the project be worthwhile?

Factors to Consider in Project Assignments

- **Experience Appropriateness:** Will the student be able to process and utilize the information and resources?
- **Content:** How will the project be used to extend the learning process into a particular study area?

Remember to have peer-to-peer conferences throughout the project process so that the student is held accountable for the timeline assignments that are set. This keeps individuals from doing a project at the last minute.

PROBLEM-SOLVING MODEL

The reader identifies a problem to solve or is given a problem. It is usually related to the school, local community, or the world. The problem may be assigned to the Total group (T), a student working Alone (A), in Partner work (P), or in Small groups (S) using the TAPS model. For example:

Students identify a dangerous intersection near the community's recreation center. The teacher arranges for the students to work with a traffic engineer to gather information on regulations and requirements for installing a traffic light. The students create charts and graphs to share the information gathered.

The teacher then arranges for the class to visit the intersection to meet with the traffic engineer. The student who identified the problem reads his report to the engineer. This problem-solving technique was used in one school, and today that intersection has a traffic light.

INDEPENDENT CHOICE READING MODEL

Independent reading time provides the student with opportunities to choose a factual or fiction selection he wants to read. A supply of ready resources in the students' areas of interest is available in the classroom for selection during this time.

Some teachers allow students to bring materials from the media center, the local library, or home; these materials should have adult approval. When the reading materials are assembled, the classroom shelves will contain a variety of information relevant to the topic being studied:

- Factual information
- Fictional accounts
- Previous studies
- The current study
- A future study
- Students' areas of interest
- Readers' ability levels

Students need specific times to choose books and materials for Independent Choice Reading. This is an ideal way to encourage reading for pleasure; the student knows he can find something on the resource shelf that he cannot wait to read.

GUIDED READING MODEL

The purpose of Guided Reading is to empower students with independent reading skills and strategies they will automatically use to interpret texts and related materials. Guided Reading activities are teacher-directed learning opportunities. Conduct Guided Reading with a total class, a small group, or one student.

1. Give each student a copy of the chosen passage.

2. Present a stimulating hook to generate anticipation.

3. Introduce and teach the new vocabulary words.

4. Divide the passage into small sections.

5. Assign a section for the students to read silently and orally. The assigned passage should be on the student's personal reading level.

6. Guide and interact with the students through their reading. Each student reads the section silently. A volunteer may read it aloud.

Engage each student in sharing and discussing ideas in the passage. Ask comprehension questions to determine the students' understanding of the reading. Use questions to elicit responses that require literal, inferential, and evaluative comprehension. Present the skills through modeling, explanations, examples, and discussions during this special reading time.

In most classrooms, the Guided Reading groups form with students of similar needs. While one group works with the teacher, other students work on specific reading skills in centers, with partners, or independently. As the students' needs and strengths change, so do the individuals who make up each of the groups.

The Teacher's Role in Guided Reading

The teacher leads the students through reading passages and models using appropriate skills and strategies.

1. *Activate prior knowledge.* Use lead-ins, essential questions, graphics, music, or props to activate memories that link to the new learning, for example:

   - What do you think this is about?
   - What is going to happen?
   - Today we are going to . . .
   - How many of you remember . . . ?
   - Remember a time when. . . . ? Tell us about it.
   - Look at this picture. What does the picture tell you?
   - What do the topics and subheadings remind you of?
   - What do you think when you hear this music?

2. *Teach vocabulary* words, standards, and skills that apply to the passages.

3. *Monitor readers* and respond strategically with cues, prompts, and assistance. These aids further refine understanding of the passage.

4 *Teach students how to monitor* their comprehension and how to fix a breakdown in understanding.

5. *Model specific reasoning processes* used by effective readers to construct meaning of the text. Give students step-by-step directions to follow when completing a task. Talk through the thinking process. This demonstrates how thinking occurs during the reading process.

Sample Model for a Guided Reading Session

1. Choose the reading selection and decide on the group, using flexible grouping.

2. Select the text that matches the instructional level of the small group.

3. Get ready for reading (see page 135).

    a. Find out students' background knowledge.
    b. Arouse interest with hooks and Anticipatory Carrots.
    c. Set purposes.
    d. Make predictions.

4. Introduce the passage with pre-reading activities.

    a. Discuss the title and subheading.
    b. Preview graphics, charts, and pictures.
    c. Present the essential questions and purposes
    d. Announce the focus for teaching.

5. Introduce the new vocabulary and skills in novel ways (see Chapter 4).

    a. Analyze the structure of the word.
    b. Learn the word and the meaning used in the text.

6. Read the passage (see page 143).

    a. Assign short passages. (Some assignments call for note taking.)
    b. Students read independently.
    c. The teacher intervenes with assistance as needed.

7. Discuss and develop comprehension skills (see Chapter 6).

    a. Discuss answers to questions and facts discovered.
    b. Review organization and sequence.
    c. Redefine purpose.

8. Reread orally with small group, partner, or total group (see page 148).

9. Use the information learned to differentiate assignments for individual needs using intelligence and modality tools.

    a. Perform follow-up activities.
    b. Teach and review skills, concepts, and strategies.
    c. Locate additional information and sources.
    d. Organize learned information for creative dispalys and reports.

Assessment of Guided Reading

Use the following checklist to assess the learner's progress:

Learner Skill	Not Yet Developing	Consistent
Reads orally with expression	——	——
Knows the vocabulary	——	——
Recognizes and uses punctuation to guide reading	——	——

Demonstrates an understanding of text	————————	————————
Retells the story or information	————————	————————
Makes predictions	————————	————————
Interprets characters' feelings	————————	————————
Makes inferences	————————	————————

LANGUAGE EXPERIENCE MODEL

In a Language Experience activity, the teacher writes the student's exact words "word for word." The teacher records the statements of one or more students as they contribute thoughts to form a list, a discussion, or a story.

A Language Experience activity demonstrates the writing and reading connection. Learners observe letters forming words, the words making sentences, and sentences creating paragraphs. The Language Experience is a vital tool to use with students because they can read their own words in writing. Students often need guidance while reading. The Language Experience is effective with an individual, a small group, or a total class. Students gather near the teacher to see their words recorded and read. It is important for students to see the chart, board, paper, or computer screen as the recording of their words take place. Chart paper is easy to handle, display, move, and revisit as needed.

The teacher repeats the student's words as he models how the spoken words appear in the form of writing. Often a student does not understand that the words he says are the same words written on the paper. The teacher must explicitly demonstrate that spoken words are now in a written form. Record the student's exact words. Read each phrase as it is written. Read each sentence as it is completed. Invite students to read specific phrases and sentences. Lead the group in rereading the recorded information.

A learner may know what he wants to say but have difficulty writing it. Language Experience activities teach the student the value of writing his words as he says them. Each experience demonstrates the writing and reading connection through content lessons.

Language Experiences in the Lower Grades

The teacher usually selects the topic for a Language Experience in the lower grades. The class may choose a title before the writing begins or select a catchy, clever title when the activity is completed.

The student gives the information to the teacher orally. The teacher writes the sentence, saying the name of each letter of the word as it takes form on the chart. The teacher names the letter while writing it. The student repeats the letter's name. For example, if a student's sentence begins with the letter *T*, the teacher says, "Capital *T*." The student repeats it, saying, "Capital *T*." When the letters form a word, the teacher and the student say the word together. For example, the teacher says, "*T-h-e* spells *The*," and the student repeats it.

Using this method, the teacher reinforces each letter's name, the recognition of every word, and the connection of words to create sentences. When a sentence is complete, the teacher brings attention to each word that is read by using a pointer. She reads the sentence to the listening students. The readers repeat the sentence. As each learner becomes more proficient with letter recognition, spelling, and reading, his progress is evident. His voice joins the teacher's voice as the letters and words appear in the writing.

Upon completion of a chart, the student and the teacher read the entire story, passage, or list together. The teacher reads one sentence at a time and asks the student to repeat it. The Language Experience activity ends with an oral reading of the passage or story. It is important for the student to read and hear the words on the chart to gain an understanding of the writing and reading connection. The teacher points to each word as it is being read. The pointer moves along with a continuous flow while reading. Use the same process when a student is in the early stages of composing journal stories.

Language Experiences in the Upper Grades

Language Experience activities are effective for conveying topic information in the upper grades. A chart, blackboard, overhead, or computer projection screen is used to record student responses during a small group or class discussion. The teacher reads each word, sentence, or phrase after writing it. This repetition reinforces word recognition and correct spelling.

Any time a teacher records a student's words, it is a Language Experience. This technique is used when the teacher records the responses of students to questions during class discussions. For example, a student realizes that as he speaks the teacher is scripting his words. When he needs to respond to an open-ended question on a test, he realizes that he needs to write the words in his thoughts as he would say them orally. Often, a student knows the answers but does not know how to transfer his information to tests. Language Experience activities develop metacognitive skills the reader needs to record his thoughts.

A big mistake teachers often make as they record the statements of students is to misinterpret the students' information as they are writing it. The teacher must continually ask for clarification, because if the teacher writes misinterpreted information, the student may not volunteer to correct the teacher.

Figure 3.3   Adjustable Assignment for Language Experience

• Can write and read the story • Is a leading contributor to the Language Experience process • Has a strong knowledge base of language and sentence construction • Spells the word before the teacher writes it • Is a fluent, comprehending reader	• Contributes to the story or topic • Recognizes and knows how to spell most common words • Reads most of the words without assistance	• Repeats letters and words after the teacher • Reads a few words without assistance
High Degree of Mastery	Approaching Mastery	Beginning

Adapted from Gregory and Chapman, 2002a

The teacher also should encourage the student to speak up with further explanations. If the information is not clear, ask the student probing questions. Probing questions and statements elicit explanations that usually clarify the previous statement. Examples of these include:

- Tell me more.
- What part do you not understand?
- Explain this . . .
- What does _____mean?

Create a risk-free environment, so each student feels free to express himself. Let the student know that it is important for everyone in the class to know and understand the meaning of his statements and comments. Clear communication lines are vital to productive work with all Language Experience activities (see Figure 3.3).

SHARED READING MODEL

During Shared Reading experiences, everyone has an individual copy of the passage selected for the activity. The students gather around the teacher. The passage selection is important to make this activity successful. The pupils follow along the words as the teacher reads to them. Students who know how to read some words join in the reading. During the Shared Reading strategy, the teacher provides needed word prompts and cues. Passages are reread and retold (Brown & Cambourne, 1990).

Guidelines for Shared Reading

1. Choose an appropriate selection with interesting, intriguing topic information.

2. Use books with predictable language such as a rhyme, rhythm, or repetitive phrases.

3. Begin with an exciting hook to get the group interested in reading related topic information.

4. Let the students make predictions about the selection.

5. Read the passage aloud.

6. Discuss the selection.

   - Ask students to give the information in their own words.
   - Elicit and confirm predictions.
   - Describe the details and valuable descriptive information.

7. Repeat the reading using various reading designs.

   - Assign parts for the students to read with the teacher.
   - Ask students to join in the parts they are able to read.

8. Provide a follow-up experience.

During Shared Reading experiences, students see the connection between written and spoken forms of language. They learn to read a book from front to back. They see that print runs from left to right and from top to bottom. They observe the teacher as reading is modeled. As listeners, they hear the story read with expression and fluency. As the book or selection is read repeatedly, students further develop their listening and sight vocabulary. The discussions and follow-up activities teach readers that meaning comes from print.

READ ALOUD MODEL

Read Aloud experiences give students of all ages the opportunity to hear the sounds and rhythms of the language. Each child needs someone to read to him every day. Jim Trelease, author of *The Read Aloud Handbook* (2001), says that if every person were read to orally every day from the time he was born until he was twenty-two years old, we would have a literate world.

Figure 3.4   Suggested Read Aloud materials

Books	Articles	Others
Picture	Newspaper	Trivia
Fiction	School news	Quotes
Factual	Magazines	Sayings
Text		

Read aloud to students each day. Make reading aloud a daily routine in all classrooms, in all subjects, and in all grade levels. Choose passages that relate to the topic of study or a high-interest area. The Read Aloud time gives the student the opportunity to see and hear a reading model. There is a pleasure gained from listening to a model reader. When adults read aloud to students, they show their passion for the piece through their emotions, voice inflections, and feelings. Relationships of letters to words, words to phrases, phrases to sentences, and sentences to paragraphs are better understood, especially if the listener is looking at the printed material as it is being read aloud.

THE FOUR BLOCK MODEL

The Four Block planning format teaches reading in an organized manner covering vocabulary development, guided reading, independent reading, and writing. Each block consists of a 60- to 90-minute time period. A section of each reading component is taught during each allotted block of time.

Some instruction is conducted with the total group; for example, the entire class may need to hear the directions and the introductory hook. Some reading skills and strategies develop as the student works alone. Students need time to work alone to create their own interpretations of the information they read. Other times students find a comfortable place to work with a reading partner. Often instruction leads to small group work; for example, the teacher may lead a group in a guided reading lesson. Guided Reading sessions provide opportunities to model reading, to teach skills, to assess, and to apply thinking skills.

Flexible grouping is implemented to tap into preferences and potential of diverse learners. The Four Block method is a structured way to strategically plan reading instruction. With appropriate activities in each quadrant, fluent, comprehending readers are developed through well-planned, meaningful lessons.

Figure 3.5   Four Block

Vocabulary Development	Guided Reading
Purposes • To introduce, assess, and review vocabulary words • To decode words in content • To work with structural analysis clues • To apply phonics automatically • To master sight words • To teach various learning strategies Examples: Draw or act out the meaning • To master content words for personal ownership	**Purposes** • To read a wide range of fiction and nonfiction materials related to the topic • To model and teach comprehension strategies and skills • To teach from a text, or from multiple copies of a trade book or literature (factual/fictitious) • To teach reading skills and tools • To check for understanding of passages • To read various genres related to the topic • To use different levels of thinking to check for understanding • To use explicit, inference, and evaluative questions • To develop the ability to identify the author's purpose, main ideas, and supporting details • To identify problems and find solutions
Independent Reading	Writing
Purposes • To select and read personal reading materials • To practice reading • To develop an eager, fluent reader • To develop opportunities to read a variety of materials chosen by the learner • To read text assignments alone • To read at their own pace • To comprehend and interpret information • To find a personal fit: If I need it, I retain it • To read materials in areas of interest	**Purposes** • To respond and interpret in written form to the information read • To record thoughts on paper • To express points of view and draw conclusions • To use different types of writing to respond to reading Examples: expository, narrative, descriptive, persuasive • To use various genres Examples: lists, editorials, songs

FROM MODELS TO IMPLEMENTATION

The following differentiated instructional strategies include agendas, cubing, response books, graphic organizers, and choice boards to use with content material. The flexibility of each activity provides options to meet the reader's individual needs during the implementation of a specific reading model.

AGENDAS/MENUS

An agenda is a list of tasks for an individual or a small group of students to do during independent work time. Often while students are working on their agenda lists, a teacher is working with a small group, assisting students, or assessing individual learners.

Sometimes the agenda is presented to the student in a folder. Tasks on the list must be completed in a specified time, for example, during a particular unit of study students are assigned a work folder, and it is due on a certain day of the study. Many students can have the same assignments because they share similar knowledge, interests, or ability levels.

Agendas are an organizational tool for planning instruction that allows each student to work at his own level. An agenda can be used with any age student in any subject area across the curriculum. There are usually three groups or less. This means that small groups of students can have the same items on their assignment list. The agenda is determined by individual need and knowledge base.

The teacher assesses progress along the way. As part of the information in the folder, the students can be given an agenda log (see Figure 3.6) or an agenda checklist (Figure 3.7). The student can record each entry at the end of a work session. Agendas are often referred to as "menus."

Why Use Agendas?

- **Pacing:** A student works at his own pace. The student learns to use his time wisely. The learner has a deadline to complete all tasks assigned. The individual learner paces himself. He is allotted adequate time to work effectively and efficiently on each task. The student is his own time manager.
- **Sequence:** The student determines the order to complete the agenda items. One student may complete the easiest tasks first while another student may complete difficult tasks first.
- **Independence:** Agendas foster independence. A student who is working on an agenda is accepting responsibility. He works independently and is in charge of completing the assignment.

Figure 3.6   Sample agenda log

Date	Today I	I need help on	Item and completion date	Comments

Figure 3.7   Sample agenda checklist

Student _____   Topic, Subject, or Unit _____

Date of Assignment _____   Due Date _____

TASK	A	B	C	D
Task or assignment				
Beginning work date				
Completion date				
What I learned				
Request for assistance				
Concerns and questions				
Comments				

Check Points   Identification _____ Signature _____ Date _____
                Identification _____ Signature _____ Date _____
                Identification _____ Signature _____ Date _____
                Identification _____ Signature _____ Date _____

Identification
S: Self
C: Classmate
P: Parent
T: Teacher

Figure 3.8 Agenda ideas

Reading Related Material	Computer Activities	Art Project	Logical Thinking	Reenactment	Hands-on Learning	Listening and Viewing
Take notes on the material.	Gather research on the Web.	Create a collage or mobile.	Write what you learned.	Make a simulation, example, or demonstration.	Use a manipulative.	Listen to a tape, CD, or recording.
Plot the information on a graphic organizer.	Create a PowerPoint presentation.	Make a mural.	Develop a timeline.	Write an interview for one of the story characters.	Do an experiment.	View a video.
Create a fact sheet about the passage.	Create a word document about the topic.	Make a diorama.	Write the step-by-step procedure.	Role-play a character or a scene.	Follow an assembly line or recipe.	Read with a partner.
Learn unit vocabulary words.	Solve a crossword or word puzzle.	Develop a poster.	Solve a puzzle or problem.	Write a play about the reading.	Play a game.	Write with a partner.
Create a sequence board with the information.	Play an educational game.	Sculpt a character.	Answer questions on the topic.	Act out the meaning of the vocabulary words or key concepts.	Create an exhibit.	Participate in a text talk.
	Use a purchased Computer program.	Build a setting or example.	Adapt the information for a practical experience.		Work in the center.	Join a literary circle.
	Design a graphic.	Illustrate the information or procedure.				View a reenactment.
		Develop an editorial cartoon.				
		Draw the scene of the event.				
		Illustrate the meanings of a vocabulary word or concept.				

- **Time on Task:** Agenda assignments provide independent practice and growth on individual skills and learning in needed content. They eliminate busy work and foster efficient and quality use of time on essential needs.

How Are Agendas Used?

- The teacher assigns all tasks.
- The teacher assigns some tasks and the student chooses others from a Choice Board or a list of agenda ideas (see Figure 3.8). For example:

  1. The teacher assigns 1–3 tasks.
  2. The student chooses 2–4 tasks from the Choice Board.

- The student chooses teacher-designed tasks from the Choice Board.
- The student chooses from the teacher-designed Choice Board and also uses a Wild Card to design a learning activity related to the topic. *Note:* The Wild Card should be submitted by the student to the teacher for approval.

CUBING

Cubing is a learning strategy that provides opportunities for students to use and share their thinking in relation to a topic, subject, or unit of study. Each side of the cube is labeled with a direction that uses the information gained from reading the text or related materials. Cubes may be color-coded to reflect diverse learning abilities. For example, an orange cube may contain directions for struggling readers while a blue cube may contain directions for readers who need a challenge. Use the cubing activities to add novelty to processing information.

Cubing activities can strengthen strengths. If a student has difficulty understanding a skill or concept, incorporate the learner's abilities or strengths to learn the skill. For example, a student with musical abilities may learn the skill if he uses it in a song, rap, or poetry. These cubing activities can also strengthen weaknesses. Design cubing activities that provide successful experiences in the learner's area of weakness. Cubing activities can be fun, interesting and stimulating to learners. They teach and challenge problem solving and thinking (see Figure 3.9).

Variations

- Number the list. Roll the dice to select the item on the list to complete.
- Write each direction on a small strip of construction paper. Mix the strips. Ask each student to draw a strip.

Figure 3.9 Cube Examples

Thinking Cube 1	*Thinking Cube 2*
1. Analyze	1. List
2. Plot	2. Describe
3. Compare	3. Argue
4. Contrast	4. Apply
5. Define	5. Conclude
6. Support	6. Discuss
Visual /Spatial Cube	*Bodily/Kinesthetic Cube*
1. Design a poster	1. Create a dance.
2. Create a graphic	2. Role-play.
3. Color code.	3. Design a manipulative.
4. Make a collage.	4. Build a model.
5. Create a banner.	5. Play charades.
6. Design an ad.	6. Create a celebration.
Intelligences Cube 1	*Intelligences Cube 2*
1. Illustrate (Draw)	1. Write a summary.
2. Plot information	2. Create a game.
3. Role-play.	3. Use a manipulative
4. Create a poem.	4. Create a poster
5. Take a stand.	5. Develop a song.
6. Compare it with your world.	6. Reflect in a journal.

- Apply various levels of questioning as outlined on Bloom's taxonomy.
- Examples:
  Find the word that means _____. (Knowledge level)
  How is this information valuable to our community? (Evaluation level)
- Incorporate learning styles in the reading activities.
  Example for the concrete learner:
  Design a model to demonstrate the _____

On the Flip Side

Divide the class into 3-member teams.

1. Give each team 5 pieces of paper for the question cards. Use a different shape for each team.

2. Assign a section of the text to each team.

3. Encourage the team to find a comfortable place to read and work.

4. Direct the team to create 5 important questions with their answers.

5. Write a question on one side of each card.

6. Write the answer on the other side of one of the other questions. Note: The answer must be written on the back of another question.

7. Mix the cards together and distribute to the class.

8. Students take turns reading the question on the cards.

9. The student with the correct answer says, "Flip Side"

10. He reads the correct answer and the question on the Flip Side.

11. If the answer is incorrect, repeat the initial question until the correct answer is given.

Variation

Review with the Flip Side Card game. Use the cards later in a center.

RESPONSE BOOKS

Plan content assignments for reviews using different formats of book designs and shapes, textures of paper, writing fonts, and implements. Use these projects to create interest during a unit of study. Figure 3.10 offers suggestions for the students.

1. Shape Books

   a. Choose a shape from the unit being studied.
   b. Cut several pages of the same shape and staple the pages together.

2. Mobiles

   a. Use a hanger to create a mobile that reflects the information being learned.

3. Shoe Box Reports

   a. In a shoe box place a word, picture, question, or object that is part of the lesson to create a mystery.

   b. Decorate the outside of the box with key phrases, words, and visuals related to the mystery as clues.
   c. Show the answer after many guesses

Figure 3.10 Response books (Illustrations by Richard Venard Willis)

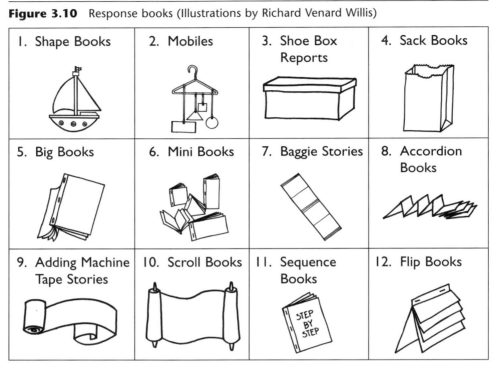

1. Shape Books	2. Mobiles	3. Shoe Box Reports	4. Sack Books
5. Big Books	6. Mini Books	7. Baggie Stories	8. Accordion Books
9. Adding Machine Tape Stories	10. Scroll Books	11. Sequence Books	12. Flip Books

Adapted from Gregory and Chapman, 2002a

4. Sack Books

    a. Decorate the outside of the sack about the topic, book, chapter, character, or event.

    b. Place related artifacts and props inside the sack.

    c. Use the sack as presentation props.

5. Big Books

    a. Attach large sheets of paper together to make a book.

    b. Design a cover with the title.

    c. Create the book pages.

    d. Assign one page to each student or to each cooperative group to complete in the sequence of an event, a story, an experiment, or a timeline.

    e. Place an extra page in the back for all participating class members to sign as authors.

6. Mini Books

   a. Instead of Big Books, Mini Books can be excellent to use when trying to remember small bits of information.
   b. Instead of entire sequences as in Big Books, place one graphic, procedural step, vocabulary word, or picture on each page.

7. Baggie Stories

   a. Get a zippered plastic bag for each cooperative group in the classroom.
   b. Cut each bag down both sides and open it out flat.
   c. Zip the bags together, and place a mark at the top of the side of the flattened bag that the students will write on.
   d. Pass out one bag per cooperative group.
   e. Each group is assigned one element, attribute, fact, detail, step, or passage of the assignment.
   f. Have the students read the assignment.
   g. Ask students to draw a picture on the top part of the bag to illustrate the important part to remember.
   h. Students write about the picture and what is needed to retain on the bottom part of the bag.
   i. Decide the order that the groups will present the information.
   j. Gather the bags and zip them together in the order decided to form a continuous line.
   k. Each group goes to the overhead and presents their part on their bag as it rolls across the overhead.

8. Accordion Books

   a. Fold the paper in and out like an accordion.
   b. Write a step in the procedure on each page.
   c. The cover can become an animal or person shape by adding a face, hands, and feet.

9. Adding Machine Tape Stories

   a. Write a story starter, a key vocabulary word, or a topic on the beginning of a long piece of machine tape.
   b. Pass the tape from person to person; each one adds to the story.
   c. Each writer must add to what has already been written. Therefore, he must read the information and continue with the topic and thought.

10. Scroll Books

   a. Roll a sheet of parchment on two dowel rods, sticks, rulers, or pencils.
   b. Write and draw on the scroll.

11. Sequence Books

   a. Choose a topic that has a step-by-step procedure.
   b. Put one step, with an explanation, on each page of the book.
   c. Encourage students to go through the book page by page and make sure there has been no ignored step.
   d. Check to see that no step is ignored.

   Examples: Training manual, Assembly manual, Experiment log, Recipes

12. Flip Books. Refer to illustration 12 on page 79.

GRAPHIC ORGANIZERS

When a learner uses graphic organizers to plot information, he interprets what he has read in a personal way. Explain each organizer so it becomes a user-friendly tool for the student's independent use. Here are some guidelines to use when teaching graphic organizer skills.

Teacher's Role in Teaching Graphic Organizers

Model Their Use Across Disciplines The teacher needs to model the use of each graphic organizer by plotting information on it repeatedly with different topics. For example, when comparing and contrasting, use a Venn diagram. This can be used across disciplines with any subject. In a history lesson, compare and contrast two major battles. In language arts class, compare authors or stories. In science class, compare invertebrates and vertebrates. A learner sees how the same graphic organizer works in different situations. He sees the techniques and various ways to use a particular organizer. The reader develops a new tool to add to his study repertoire.

Use It in Different Formats

Let the student explore ways to use the drawings, so he learns to use them as comfortable learning tools. For example, an Idea Tree is a great tool to teach cause and effect. In another situation, this same organizer may become a mind map. For example, challenge students to compare three items using three intersecting circles or designs as they organize information.

*Use the Same
Information on Different Organizers*

One group of students can choose a mind map to plot the information learned on a topic, another may choose a fish bone for the same data, and

Figure 3.11 Graphic organizers (Illustrations by Richard Venard Willis)

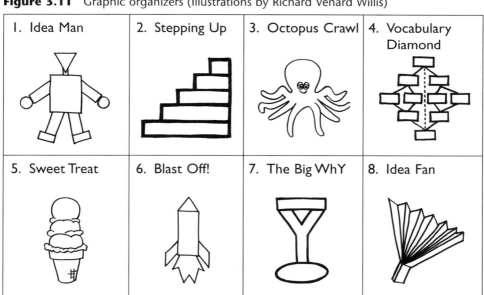

Adapted from Gregory and Chapman, 2002a

another a rocket ship. By learning about different organizers to plot data, the students can pick and choose the one that works best for them (see Figure 3.11).

Ways to Use Graphic Organizers

Idea Man: Studying a Character

1. Put the name of a factual or fictitious character in the head triangle.
2. Brainstorm attributes details, facts, or thoughts about the person on the body lines. *Note:* Add as many as needed.
3. Place the conclusion, summary, or critique of the character on the legs and feet.

Stepping Up: Sequential Order

1. Place the topic or concept on the top of the ladder.
2. Write the procedural directions or sequence of an event on the ladder in sequential order.
3. Start at the top and move down the ladder. Use one step in the procedure or process on each ladder step.

Octopus Crawl: Brainstorming

1. Write the essential question or topic to brainstorm on the body of the octopus.

2. Place each idea brainstormed about the subject on a separate tentacle of the octopus.

Vocabulary Diamond: Word Associations

1. Write a word from the unit of study in the top box on Line A.

2. On Line B, write a different word that relates to the Line A word in each of the two boxes.

3. In the first two boxes on Line C, write the first two words that you think of when you say the Line B word. Repeat the same process for the other boxes on that line.

4. Look at the two word sets in Line D. Place an associated word under each set of words.

5. Write a word that links to line D in the last box.

6. Draw a line in the middle of the graphic from the top word to the bottom word. Write many ways these two terms are alike.

Sweet Treat! Attributes

1. Place a scene, character, main idea, or event on the cone.

2. Put an attribute, fact, or detail about it in each scoop of ice cream

Blast Off! Cause and Effect

1. State the problem in the top or cone part of the rocket.

2. Place the causes on each the lines from the fuel injection.

3. Place the effects on the center part of the rocket.

The Big WhY? Problems and Solutions

1. State a problem, hypothesis, or essential question in the box.

2. Write solutions on three stems of the Y.

3. Write your conclusion in the oval.

Idea Fan: Main Idea and Supporting Details

1. Write the main idea on the line.

2. Write supporting details on each line of the fan.

CHOICE BOARDS

Choice Boards offer flexible learning strategies to use with the reading models. For example, the teacher may ask the reader to select one or more projects or problem solving activities from the board. A student usually appreciates opportunities to play a major role in task decisions. Remember to design the board activities to teach or reinforce content information and meet the reader's needs. See pages 26, 27, 162 and 163 for a variety of choice board ideas.

SUMMARY

Teachers who are aware of their students' diverse needs know how to create checklists, surveys, inventories, or other assessment tools that match the reader's needs with the learning. After collecting the assessment data, teachers can chart the course for a segment of the reading journey.

The models of reading detailed in this chapter can guide instruction. The teacher selects and adapts the model that coordinates the reader's needs with content standards and learning objectives. The Adjustable Assignment model is a planning tool, because the reader's current knowledge on a topic is recorded with the information listed that he needs to know.

The Models of Reading provide engaging formats for reading sessions in the content areas. The Adjustable Assignment Model is a planning tool that utilizes the reader's knowledge base as the foundation for learning. If a reader is identified as being on or above the mastery level, the teacher may select and adapt one of the models to customize the reading activities for the learner. For example, use the Curriculum Compacting Model, a Project Based Model or the Problem Solving Model to meet the student's unique needs.

Step-by-step procedures for reading experiences are outlined in the Guided Reading Model, the Language Experience Model, and the Shared Reading Model. Each model is designed to meet the reader's needs.

Implement the differentiated instructional strategies to enhance the reading models. The novel activities included with agendas, cubing, response books, graphic organizers, and choice boards use content information to challenge and intrigue the reader.

Vocabulary 4

The authors designed this chapter to help teachers create vocabulary learning opportunities that meet the diverse needs of all learners in the differentiated classroom.

Subject Terminology

Each content area has key words the reader needs to know and understand. Many of those words require students to use higher-order thinking. Choose key words to post. It is also important to vary the terms used in directions when making written and oral assignments. The ability to use and understand terms in directions is vital for success on assignments and tests in each subject area.

Do not assume a student knows the subject's vocabulary terms just because he was introduced to the words in previous lessons. It is common for a learner to recall a word, know how to pronounce it, but lack the understanding to apply the word in the new context. Create a checklist of subject-related terms that students are expected to master. The following is a sample list of terms readers need to know related to math:

Math Terms Found in Directions

add	describe	list	replace
answer	develop	locate	report
calculate	devise	maintain	review
change	diagram	mark	round
check	divide	match	select
choose	do	measure	sequence
choreography	draw	multiply	show
classify	estimate	name	simplify
compare	explain	note	solve
complete	figure	plan	support
compose	find	predict	subtract

compute	formulate	prescribe	teach
conduct	give	prepare	tell
construct	graph	practice	think
contrast	group	rank	trace
copy	hypothesize	rationalize	use
create	identify	read	work
debate	illustrate	regroup	write
define	line up		

LEARNING NEW WORDS

An effective way to reach individual learners is to relate each new vocabulary word to the students' background knowledge and experiences. Use strategies and activities to make links and connections between the content material and the learner's world.

The mind likes unsolved mysteries, challenges, and discoveries. Treat the introduction of a vocabulary word as an adventure by creating anticipation and excitement. This phase of learning is important, because the desire to learn a new word is easily turned on or off during this stage of the lesson. Select words wisely. Maintain the reader's interest with a variety of exciting, novel strategies that focus attention on the word.

Vocabulary words for the student to learn are selected from the content lesson. The typical way a word is taught is to ask the student to do the following:

1. Look at the word.

2. Hear the word.

3. Pronounce the word with the teacher.

4. Spell it.

5. Write it.

6. Look it up in the dictionary. And,

7. Write a sentence using the word.

What is wrong with this method? It is not wrong. It is one effective way to introduce a new word to students, but it is not the only way. If this method is overused, the activity becomes a routine procedure and a mundane, non-thinking task. This has become the vocabulary rut of today's classrooms. But learners in the differentiated reading classroom need to work with many strategies to learn new words. A variety of strategies and activities add novelty to each learning experience.

Sight Vocabulary

The terms "sight vocabulary" and "sight words" are easily confused. An individual's *sight vocabulary* includes all the words he recognizes without effort. Rehearse the pronunciation and meaning of the word in different ways until the reader uses it automatically. The student knows a word when it becomes a part of his social language and inner speech or self-talk. *Sight words* are words that do not conform to our common pronunciation guides. They "do not play by the rules." Words such as *of, to,* and *you* are sight words (Gipe, 2002).

When a learner is introduced to a new word, he places it in short-term memory. By using, applying, and adapting the word to units and lessons in the content areas, the learner puts the word in long-term memory. If the experience is meaningful, useful, and purposeful for the reader, he is more apt to retain the word. To own a word, the student needs a personal connection with the word and its meaning.

Procedure for Learning a New Word

Each classroom has a diverse group of learners with diverse needs. Individuals learn vocabulary in different ways. If readers are expected to learn and retain a word, the teacher must introduce and teach the word in a variety of ways. A good way to start is with ideas from a Learn a Word Choice Board (see Figure 4.1) that can guide the student to work further with the word.

Assign a word to each student. Assign or ask the students to choose a way to teach the word to others from the Learn a Word Choice Board (see Figure 4.1), working with partners or in small groups. Call on volunteers to share some of their favorites with the total class.

Word Discovery

Use a discovery method to add novelty to a vocabulary lesson. For example, introduce a word as a mystery. This strategy helps the reader learn how to use clues to discover word meanings. Write the word on the board; have the class pronounce it. Use the following directions to challenge the class:

1. Post the word.

2. Find the new word in a scavenger hunt in the selected passage.

3. Give a "thumbs up" when it is found.

4. Read the word.

5. Read the sentences surrounding the word.

Figure 4.1   Learn a Word Choice Board

Connect the word with something in the student's world and discuss it.	Locate the word in the text, and read the paragraph to get context meaning.	Create a design that depicts the meaning of the word.
Make a mnemonic to remember the word and its meaning.	Make a word puzzle or a game.	Contrast the word with something else.
Write a poem with the word, its meaning, and facts about the word. Illustrate it.	Tell a story using the word three times in the plot.	Teach the word and its meaning in a memorable way to a classmate.
Explain how the word is used in the text.	Divide the word into syllables. Chant and tap syllables.	Create a song, poem, cheer, or rap using the word as the topic.
Role play the meaning.	Design a banner or flag for the word.	Sell the word by writing an ad for it.

Variation

When students are able to find the chosen word in several places in the text, create partners or small groups to share the word, the meaning, and various ways it is used in each location.

Mystery Word

This activity builds anticipation, curiosity, and excitement for learning a new word. Use the strategy several days before the unit begins to entice learners to investigate and discover new words.

1. From the topic, choose a key word that is unknown.

2. Post the key word using large, visually attractive letters.

3. Use the following questions to stimulate thinking in relation to the posted word.

   - What will we learn about this new word?
   - Why is this word used?
   - How does it fit into our new unit of study?

Variation 1

Choose a key word from an upcoming unit one week before the introduction of the word. Add one letter of the word to the posting each day and challenge students to guess the word. Provide a space around the posting for the students to write their guesses.

Variation 2

Post an unfamiliar key word from a unit of study. Post a new clue each day and have the students guess the meaning of the word.

Variation 3

Write the key word from the unit of focus on a large card. Example:

Key word: region

Students write each fact they know about the term on an individual sticky note. Have students brainstorm words or phrases related to the term. Write the responses under or beside the key word to create a Visual Associations list or definition for each word. This is a pre-assessment tool to determine students' prior knowledge related to the word. Examples:

fractions:	numerator	denominator	proper	improper
Greece:	Parthenon	gods	goddesses	ruins
topography:	isthmus	prairie	mountain	peninsula

STUDENT MASTERY OF VOCABULARY

Often the teacher says, "But I taught that word." The student needs to think, "Did I learn that word?" Vocabulary knowledge is vital to understanding during reading experiences.

A reader must know various ways to learn and remember new words in all subjects. Vocabulary words may be general or they may be content-specific, technical terms, but they must be placed into the learner's world and made personally relevant.

The Word *Vocabulary*

Give students a simple definition of the word *vocabulary,* such as "a word that is read or said and used easily in the right place." For example, write the word *vocabulary* with the word *vocal* directly below it. Underline

Figure 4.2 Adjustable Assignment for vocabulary introduction. A: What they know. B: What they need next. C: How to teach this group.

	High Level of Mastery	Approaching Mastery	Beginning Mastery
C How to teach this group	• Write a story using the word in a different genre. Read the story to a classmate. • Create a word puzzle with the word. (See "A Word on Words") • Develop a word game to play with a partner. • Design a word web with related words. • Evaluate the word's value to the topic. Write a sales pitch to sell the word to a publisher for a dictionary.	• Use the word in a skit or cartoon. • Review the word in the glossary, word list, chart, diagram, and text passage. • Illustrate the meaning for a word wall. • Create a memory device for the word. • Reread the passage using a synonym or phrase to replace the word.	• Show pictures with the word's meanings. • Give each word a debut. • Read easy passages that contain the word. • Say each syllable and repeat several times. • Teach memory tricks and gimmicks for the word. • Act the Word: Say it, give the definition, and an action to illustrate the meaning. • Plan activities for reader interaction with the word, such as cutting it out, pasting it, and designing it.
B What they need next	• Needs praise for knowing the word • Needs to know how to use and apply the words in varied ways	• Needs ownership of the word • Needs a novel way to learn the word • Needs to be able to analyze context clues	• Needs an effective introduction of the word to own the word • Needs to learn word's meaning • Needs opportunities to adapt the word for personal use
A What they know	• Reads the word automatically • Knows the word's meaning • Uses the word correctly in context	• Has some knowledge of the word • Recognizes the word • Has no recall of the meaning	• Has no knowledge of the word • Has little knowledge of the word

Adapted from Gregory and Chapman, 2002a

the first four letters in each word to illustrate that the base word means "voice." Discuss the many meanings of the term until it's clear that students understand it.

The student's mastered vocabulary consists of all of the words in his command. When the learner understands a word's use and knows how to apply it properly, he owns the word. The student's mastered vocabulary may include:

- The words a person pronounces and uses correctly to communicate through speaking, reading, thinking, and writing
- A word list in alphabetical order
- The words in a language
- The words related to a subject or topic

Adjustable Assignments for Learning New Vocabulary

Each student has a different knowledge base in relation to each new word. Through experiences, the learner builds his own repertoire of knowledge related to the topic. In planning differentiated vocabulary learning, an Adjustable Assignments model can be adapted to any subject or grade level across the curriculum (Gregory & Chapman, 2002a).

Figure 4.2 shows the knowledge base level of a group of students introduced to a set of vocabulary words for a unit of study. There are three columns to reflect three levels of mastery. The student who has little or no prior experience with the content words is at the Beginning Mastery level. Many students in the class have some knowledge of the word. This group is at the Approaching Mastery level. The student who knows the word and uses it appropriately in his reading, writing, and language is working at the High Level of Mastery. Plan vocabulary lessons appropriate to the student's instructional level or zone of proximal development (Vygotsky et al., 1978; Vygotsky, 1986).

The mind can retain seven chunks of information in short-term memory. Introduce seven words at one time to get information into the students' short-term memory. After the words are introduced, they can be used in varied ways during the unit of study until they become a part of long-term memory, as words that are automatic or mastered by the learner. This develops learner ownership of the word.

PRACTICAL VOCABULARY STRATEGIES AT WORK

A student must have a strong vocabulary to become a fluent reader. The strategies in this section teach vocabulary skills using key words in the content information. The games and activities are student-friendly and practical. They engage the student's intelligences and learning modalities. Teachers can meet the diverse needs of each reader in their classrooms through these differentiated strategies that can be adapted to the content of the lesson.

Pre-assessing Knowledge Base of the Word

Find out which words on the unit vocabulary list the students already know. This way the teacher can strategically plan and teach the needed words for the individual, small group, or total class groups that do not know the word or need further instruction. Pre-assessment is the key.

Pre-assessment 1: Color My World

Teach the student to use the Color My World strategy to label vocabulary words in the text, lists, notes, or fact sheets. This strategy shows the student the value of self-monitoring his vocabulary knowledge. Provide the student with sticky tabs, highlighters, crayons, colored dots, or pencils in varying colors. This activity is an ideal assessment to determine the student's knowledge base of the vocabulary word list. The reader marks new vocabulary words following these directions:

- Green   (Go)   I know this word and use it with ease.
- Yellow   (Caution)   I know a little about this word.
- Red   (Stop)   I do not know this word.

Pre-assessment 2: Meet and Greet!

This activity shows the teacher and the student the words that need more work for mastery. It gives each student a sense of responsibility as he analyzes his personal knowledge of each word.

- Post a word list from a new unit of study.
- Have students fold a sheet of paper into a burrito (tri-) fold.
- Ask the students to write the headings shown in Figure 4.3 as titles for each section of their papers.
- Place each vocabulary word in the appropriate column.

Pre-assessment 3: Box It!

The Box It strategy (Figures 4.4 and 4.5) illustrates the structural parts of a vocabulary word. It provides an opportunity for the learner to use the

Figure 4.3 Meet and Greet new words

Words I know	Words I have seen or heard but do not use	Words I have never seen or heard.

new word in meaningful ways. A base word (for example, *lock*) is a word that stands alone without losing its meaning when a prefix (*un*-lock) or suffix (lock-*ing*) is added. The Box It activity also can be used to introduce new words with other categories, for example:

- A joke
- A slogan
- A rhyme
- A song title
- A unique connection

Teaching the Word

Words in Motion

The Words in Motion activity is an easy, fun way to learn new words. This strategy teaches word meanings through body movement or actions. Look through the vocabulary list, and choose a group of seven words with meanings that lend themselves to bodily motion. Try the following activity (adapted from Chapman & King, 2000) with each word:

Figure 4.4 Box It strategy

Choose a word with a prefix and a suffix.		
Write the prefix.	Write the base or root word.	Write the suffix.
Create a design.	Write the definition.	Create a sentence.

Figure 4.5 Box It example

Unlocking		
un	lock	ing
	Removal of a fastener	He is unlocking the door with a gold key.

1. Look at the word and pronounce it.
2. Say the meaning.
3. Choose a motion to match the meaning.
4. Pronounce the word. Say the meaning with the motion.
5. Repeat Step 4 three times.

Vocabulary Beat!

Vocabulary Beat is a strategy that teaches students how to remember words and their meanings by using them with a beat or a rhythm. Discuss musical jingles and rhymes in well-known commercials. Ask students to make up vocabulary versions. Remind students that if they choose to create a song they should use a familiar tune. This way the class's concentration will be on the content information rather than the tune of the song. Ask the class to join together in a vocabulary performance activity:

1. Divide the class into groups.
2. Assign a new vocabulary word to each group for the word debut.
3. Ask each group to create a rap, jingle, chant, poem, or song for the new word.
4. The students present their words in a vocabulary performance.

Take the focus vocabulary and write a song. Here are some Chapman and King classics:

Example 1: Planet study

Tune: "Row, Row, Row Your Boat"
Planets, planets, we will name
From closest to the sun.
Mercury, Venus, Earth, and Mars
Now we have begun.

Planets, planets, we will name,
The Solar System's for me.
Jupiter, Saturn, and Uranus.
They're the middle three.

Planets, planets, we will name,
Revolve around the sun.
Neptune and Pluto are next in line.
Explore planet fun.

Mercury, Venus, then comes Earth
With Mars and Jupiter too,
Saturn, Uranus, Neptune, Pluto.
I named the planets. Can you?

—Chapman and King, 2003

Example 2: Coin study

Tune: "Are You Sleeping?"

A penny is worth one cent.   A nickel is worth five cents.
A penny is worth one cent.   A nickel is worth five cents.
A copper coin.   A round silver coin.
A copper coin.   A round silver coin.
One, two, three, four.   Five, ten, fifteen, twenty.
One, two, three, four.   Five, ten, fifteen, twenty.

Count your pennies	Count your nickels.
Count your pennies	Count your nickels.
A dime is worth ten cents.	A quarter is worth twenty-five cents.
A dime is worth ten cents.	A quarter is worth twenty-five cents.
A tiny, silver coin.	A big silver coin.
A tiny, silver coin.	A big silver coin.
Ten, twenty, thirty, forty.	Twenty-five, fifty, seventy-five, a dollar.
Ten, twenty, thirty, forty.	Twenty-five, fifty, seventy-five, a dollar.
Count your dimes.	Count your quarters.
Count your dimes.	Count your quarters

—Chapman and King, 2003

Evening Learning Opportunity (ELO)

The Words in Motion activity can also be given as an independent assignment for homework or extra credit. This is an ideal Evening Learning Opportunity (ELO). ELOs are homework assignments that intrigue learners, interest them, and challenge their minds. They give students opportunities to work with the information and put it to a beat. Many learners are more likely to remember information when it is used in rhythmic patterns.

The Same Game

The Same Game illustrates for the student how one word and other words can have the same meaning. The activity provides an opportunity for the student to make choices, and interact with a classmate as he learns new words.

1. Choose a word from the vocabulary list that has several synonyms. Example: *boulevard*

2. Write the chosen vocabulary word with the meaning on the board or a chart.

3. Tell students to form partners and name each other A and B.

4. Partner A uses the chosen word in a sentence. Example: The boy walked down the <u>boulevard</u>.

5. Partner B repeats the sentence and replaces the vocabulary word with a synonym. Example: The boy walked down the <u>street</u>.

6. Partner A uses another synonym in the same sentence.

7. The game continues until students have used several examples.

8. Call on partner teams to give the synonyms used to make a class list under the key word.
   Examples:
   boulevard: Street, road, avenue, thoroughfare
   enormous: big, gigantic, large, huge

The Match Game

Make a deck of synonym cards for The Match Game. Place each word on a separate card from the A and B list. Examples for A/B lists:

A	B
figure	calculate
round	spherical

Divide the class in half and label the teams A and B. Give each student on the A team one word from List A. Give each student on the B team one word from List B. Ask the students to do the following:

1. Write a sentence using the word on your card.

2. Take the card and a pencil. Find a classmate with your synonym's partner.

3. Read your own sentence with the identified synonym to your partner.

4. Read each sentence substituting your partner's synonym for your word.

Match Game Variation Play the game with antonyms, homonyms, words and definitions, math symbols and their meanings, or a word with an illustration.

Artful Antics

Antonyms are words that have opposite meanings. Illustrate each word in an antonym pair with cartoons. Sample antonym pairs:

courageous/cowardly	scarce/plentiful	old/new
beginning/conclusion	rough/smooth	pain/pleasure
harmful/safe	domestic/foreign	hollow/solid
acquaintance/stranger	amateur/professional	agree/oppose

Artful Antics Variation

1. Play charades with two students acting out the meaning of each word in the antonym pair.

2. Ask the audience to guess the antonym pair.

Compound Word Wizard

A compound word is the combination of two base words to form one word. The Compound Word Wizard activity demonstrates the meaning of each word in the compound word.

1. Locate the compound word(s) in the vocabulary list.

2. Separate each word into two parts using one of the following methods:

   - Use a different color to write each part.
   - Highlight each part differently.
   - Box each word in the compound word.
   - Cut the words apart.

3. Illustrate the meaning of the compound word. Sample compound words:

   playground   pocketbook   moonlight

It Takes Two

Think of compound words that begin with the same first word. Add to these lists:

- sun: sunlight   sunglasses   sunflower   _____
- head: headrest   headset   headstrong   _____
- fire: firefly   firehouse   firefighter   _____
- air: airplane   airport   airline   _____
- door: doorway   doormat   doorstop   _____
- out: outlook   outside   outdated   _____
- side: sideswipe   sidestep   sidekick   _____

Analogy Action

An *analogy* shows the reader how words are alike or different. They provide relationships or associations between words. Analogies create meaning for the learner by making words easier to remember.

- Give several sample analogies, for example: *train* is to *track* as *car* is to *road.*

- Check to make sure the same words can be said between the two words in each analogy pair, for example: "... travels on a...."
- Draw speech bubbles between the word parts.
- Place the common words between each analogy pair in the speech bubble where the colon appears in each set of words. Examples: A train "travels on" a track :: A car "travels on" a road.

Create analogies using key vocabulary words in the content. The unknown word may appear in any position in an analogy.

Examples: Complete the word relationships in these analogies:

1. _____: messy :: young : old ["is the opposite of"]
   Choices: organized   aged   brave

2. arctic : cold :: tropics _____ ["feels"] tropics.
   Choices: hot   south   desert

3. reptile : _____ :: mammal : hairs ["covered with"]
   Choices: gills   scales   skin

Share and Compare

1. Form cooperative groups of 3–4 students.

2. Name a key word from the unit of study.

   Example: rainforest   addition   Paul Bunyan

3. Fold a large piece of newsprint into two equal sections. Label the sections A and B.

4. Instruct students to place the following in A section: The (word, phrase, or topic) is like (phrase or noun) because (reason they are alike).

   Examples:

   - The rainforest is like an umbrella because it creates a cover over the ground.
   - A trapezoid is like a rectangle because it has four sides.

   5. In the B section, illustrate the comparisons and label the common attributes.

Variation Explore contrasting attributes for the key word using the following sentence:
       _____ is not like a _____ because_____ .

Trio Masterpiece

Choose vocabulary words from the unit of focus whose meanings can be illustrated. Form groups of three and give each group three large, blank index cards.

1. One student writes the vocabulary word on a card. Underneath the word he writes the diacritical markings and part of speech.

2. The second student writes the meaning of the word on his card.

3. The third student illustrates the meaning of the word on his card.

4. The group places the same symbol on the back of each card in their set. Example: red star

5. Students pass the completed cards to the teacher.

6. The cards are shuffled and dealt to the students.

7. Each student goes on a search to find the matches for his word, definition, or illustration.

8. The trio creates a clever presentation to teach the word for the class.

9. Display the words, definitions, and illustrations by creating a vocabulary gallery.

Variation Place cards on the backs of students to create a matching game.

Crisscross Challenge

The Crisscross Challenge activity teaches students how to cross-reference vocabulary words. Try this strategy after the introduction of glossaries and other reference sections:

1. Form partners.

2. Post a vocabulary word from the text lesson.

3. Challenge partners to find the word in the chapter or unit and in the glossary or index.

4. When the team has cross-referenced the word, one student places a finger on the word he located, while his partner points to his location of the word.

5. When partners find the word in both places, they shout "Crisscross" together.

6. The partners read the information they find.

7. Keep points for each crisscross success.

T-Toon

A T-Toon is a cartoon design on a T-shirt. Ask the student to bring a plain T-shirt from home or create the design on a large piece of paper cut in the shape of a T-shirt.

1. Make a list of vocabulary words whose meanings you'll illustrate.

2. Each student chooses a favorite word from the list.

3. Use fabric pens to draw a cartoon that illustrates the word and its meaning.

   Examples:

   The following vocabulary words and definitions are from a transportation unit.

   Vehicle: Draw a picture of any means of transportation.

   Transport: Draw a picture of a vehicle carrying passengers or things.

   Passenger: Draw people or animals in a vehicle with a driver.

4. Write the key word in a jingle, advertisement, or poem on the back of the T-shirts.

5. Place synonyms in a "graffiti way" on the T-shirts.

6. Schedule a day for the student to present, wear, or display the T-Toons.

7. Display the T-Toons on a clothesline or coat hangers.

Cartoon Capers

1. Create a cartoon related to the topic using vocabulary words.

2. Write dialogue in appropriate speech bubbles.

3. Highlight or use a unique marking to identify each vocabulary word in the cartoon.

Multiple Madness

Challenge the student to create a sentence using multiple meanings of the same word. Include various forms of the word.

Examples: *fly:* Does a <u>fly</u> <u>fly</u> faster when he <u>flies</u> in an airplane?

bark: The grouchy man <u>barked</u>, "Go away" when the dog <u>barked</u> at the tree <u>bark</u>.

walk: Did you <u>walk</u> on the <u>walk</u> when he said, "Take a <u>walk</u>!"?

A Word on Words

Play this game in a center, with a small group, or as an independent assignment to practice using vocabulary words and their definitions.

1. Choose an important word from the content vocabulary list.

2. Write each letter of the key word on a separate piece of paper.

3. Arrange the letters of the word vertically on the floor.

4. Choose additional vocabulary words that have at least one letter in common with each letter in the key word. (See the example following.)

5. Write a definition clue for each word.

6. Challenge another team to solve the Word on Words puzzle.

Example 1: key word *skeleton*

a.	s _ _ _ _	It supports the upper body
b.	_ k _ _ _	Protection for the brain
c.	_ _ _ e _ _ _	Another name for the knee cap
d.	_ l _ _	A large bone in the upper arm
e.	_ _ _ _ e	The bone that causes the foot to rotate
f.	t _ _ _ _	A large bone in the lower leg
g.	_ o _ _ _	A place where two bones connect
h.	_ _ _ _ _ n _ _ _	A name for fingers and toes

Answer Key:

a. spine	b. skull	c. patella	d. ulna
e. ankle	f. tibia	g. joint	h. phalanges

Example 2: key word *train*

a.	_ t _ _	Cars ____ at the railroad crossing.
b.	r _ _	The caboose is usually ____.
c.	_ _ a _ _	The wheels of the train roll on the _____.
d.	_ _ _ i _ _	The first car on a train is the _____.
e.	_ _ _ n _ _ _ _ _ _	The _____ is the person in charge of the train.

Answer Key:

a. stop	b. red	c. track	d. engine	e. conductor

Senseless Sillies

Students enjoy becoming familiar with words through activities that are novel and humorous. Here are some challenging, fun ways to learn new words.

- Write silly sentences, stories, or riddles with the word.
- Use the word in rhymes and jingles.
- Connect the vocabulary word and the linking word in a sentence. The sentence may be silly. Often students remember silly sentences best. Challenge students to include the definition. Create a cartoon to illustrate the sentence.
- Write tongue twisters using the new words.

Example (Adapted from Burchers et al., 1997):

1. Vocabulary Word: *artery*: a vessel to carry blood

2. Linking words: artery and "are teary"

3. Connecting sentence: His eyes <u>are teary</u> because his punctured <u>artery</u> has blood flowing from it.

4. Illustration: a crying boy looking at his cut

Five Up (Adapted from the game Seven Up)

Students prepare five large cards, each with a vocabulary word on one side and the word's meaning and/or illustration on the back of the card.

1. Place the cards in a stack.

2. Call on five students to come to the front of the room.

3. The five students each draw one vocabulary card and form a line in front of the room.

4. Each student turns over his or her chosen card, so the class sees the definition.

5. The class silently reads the definitions on the five cards.

6. Each seated student places his head on his desk and closes his eyes.

7. Each student holding a card gently taps one seated student.

8. When the five students each tap someone and return to the front of the room, they say, "Five Up!"

9. Each tapped student guesses who picked him. If the first student correctly responds with the name of the person who tapped him, he must read the definition for the vocabulary word and guess the word.

10. If he answers correctly, he draws a vocabulary card and takes the place of the person who tapped him. If he guesses the word incorrectly, the student holding the card stays with the Five Up group for the next round of the game.

11. Continue the game until all vocabulary words are guessed.

Word Game Trivia

Students enjoy using topic vocabulary and trivia in popular games. Adapt these learning activities for one student, a team, or a class using a game format.
Examples:

Crosswords	Riddles	Rhymes	Concentration
Jeopardy	Wheel of Fortune	Survivor Challenges	Password
Who Wants to Be a Millionaire?		Card Games	Charades

VOCABULARY VISUALS

Create Vocabulary Visuals or word displays in various ways to grab the student's attention and maintain his interest in using the display as a reference. Form each word in a unique way and post it in a visible place or space while introducing it. For example, if the word is associated with a shape in the unit of study, ask the student to write the word on the shape. When the student creates a shape, he mentally links information to that shape. Often the selected shape depicts the meaning of the word, category, or topic. Direct the learner to add designs or features to shape patterns to make them novel.

The Vocabulary Visual can be used during a unit of study, as a bridge from one topic to another, or to review key words. Good classroom locations for visuals include:

- Backs of bookcases
- Blinds
- Bulletin boards
- Mobiles
- Ceiling
- Chart stands
- Fronts and sides of desks
- Clotheslines
- Cabinet doors
- Windows
- Window shades

The Word Wall is a popular way to display word lists. Each new word can be displayed as it is introduced. The following section provides Word Wall designs and more ideas for creating Vocabulary Visuals. Suggested activities are included.

Door Magic

1. Obtain a discarded refrigerator or vehicle door and mount it on the wall. Students enjoy these unique display items.

2. Paint or tape a decorative frame border around the door.

3. Use magnetic or colorful letters to display illustrated vocabulary words.

Base Word Wall

1. Create three columns on a bulletin board, chart, poster, or wall space.

2. Label the columns *Prefix, Base* or *Root Word,* and *Suffix.*

3. Provide paper strips, scissors, and markers in an accessible area near the Base Word Wall.

4. Challenge the student to add words to the wall by:

   • Writing the word in a colorful, graffiti way on a paper strip.
   • Cutting the word into parts: prefix, root word, and suffix.

5. Challenge the student to add words to the Base Word Wall when he meets them in his reading.

Word Substitution Wall

1. Create a chart with four columns.

2. Label the columns *Key Word, Substitute, Substitute, Substitute.*

3. Write the vocabulary word in the key word column and a synonym in the first substitute column.

4. Leave the next substitute column blank until the reader finds another synonym at a later time. Challenge students to complete the synonym columns.

Ribbon Wall

1. Hang bright, decorative ribbon from the ceiling or a hook on the wall.

2. Call on a student to staple each new word on the ribbon.

3. Connect the ribbons in creative designs.

Vocabulary Vine

Make a Vocabulary Vine to display around a bulletin board, ceiling, or door. Write key words of a topic or unit of study on leaves to attach to the vine. Call on the student to add to the vine each time you introduce a vocabulary word.

Borders

Write vocabulary words with bright colors in unique ways as special borders on bulletin boards, doorways, desks, bookcases, windows, or work areas.

Design Signs

Create a graffiti board. The learner writes the word in unique, creative ways or designs, in his graffiti way and posts it on the board. Encourage the student to use color, various media, glitter, and dots. Provide paper in various textures, sizes, and shapes. The uniqueness of the word makes it easier to remember. The student signs his designed vocabulary word.

Collection Bank

Create a personalized Word Collection Bank by alphabetizing or categorizing vocabulary words so they are easy to find and use. Create individual, personalized word banks of mastered words using one of the following:

- An index card file
- Adding machine tape
- The inside of a folder
- A box or lid
- A journal
- Bookmark
- 3-ring binder
- Necklace or chain (write a word on each link)
- Border for individual note-taking pads
- Student-made dictionary

Give Yourself a Hand

Explain that the phrase "Give him a hand" means to applaud someone. This activity provides a way for the student to "give himself a hand" for each vocabulary success.

The student writes a vocabulary word on an outline of his hand each time he discovers or learns a new word. Connect the hands with a string or ribbon. This is a form of affirmation or self-praise. Challenge the student to see how many hands he accumulates before the end of the unit or topic of study.

Know Cans

The student personalizes a can by covering it with words to describe himself. Encourage him to add designs that reflect his hobbies or special interests. When the student masters a new vocabulary word, he writes it on a slip of paper and places it in his Know Can. Conduct "canned" reviews periodically.

Stick Picks

Write each mastered vocabulary word on one side of an ice cream stick. On the other side of the stick, write the meaning or a sentence with the word. Place the Stick Picks in a small, decorated can or box. Store the sticks in categories using rubber bands or place them in envelopes for easy access. Use the Stick Picks to categorize the mastered words in the following ways:

- Alphabetically
- Common attributes
- Topic
- Subject area
- Syllables

Stomp Romp

Place new words on shoe outlines or footprints. Create a path of vocabulary words around the room, in the hallway or on the playground. The student strolls down the vocabulary path, stepping beside each word and pronouncing it.

Variation 1 Tell the student to time his vocabulary journey. Plot the time. Challenge the reader to increase his speed on each trip down the path.

Variation 2 Partners stand on each side of the first word. They hold hands high above their heads and move down the path as they say each word. Do the stroll to the beat.

Critter Crawl

Place content words on a critter that fits the topic theme. Display it from wall to wall around the work area.

Curiosity Collection Corner

Designate an area for the student to post the vocabulary words he would like to learn. Challenge the student to find words that raise his curiosity. Create a list of the words the student wants to learn. Include words he finds in various places between classes and after school. Examples:

Newspapers	Malls	Internet sites	Books	Advertisements
Videos	Labels	Sporting events	Movies	Menus
Packages	Magazines	Hallways	Neighborhood signs	
Television programs				

CUES TO CONTEXT CLUES

The word *context* means "with words." Context clues are words and phrases in a sentence that provide the meaning of an unknown word. The learner's reading level determines his ability to use context clues. When a passage contains vocabulary words that are above the student's instructional level, it is difficult for him to comprehend the text and unlock a word's meaning.

Identifying Context Clues

The following clues in a text passage often give a description, an informal meaning, or a definition for the unknown word.

Clue 1. Definition in the Text: Word Meaning

EXAMPLES:

Precipitation, a form of rain or snow, may keep us from playing outside.

His determination, or strong desire to complete his work, helped him reach his goals.

Clue 2. Synonyms: Words That Have the Same Meaning

EXAMPLES:

The enormous elephant is so large, he cannot come through our door.

The minuscule critter is so tiny, it is viewed with a magnifying glass.

Clue 3. Antonyms: Words That Are Opposites

EXAMPLES:

The rabbit was <u>fast</u>, but the <u>slow</u> turtle won the race.

Billy's mom complained about his <u>messy</u> room, so the next day it was <u>immaculate.</u>

Clue 4. Examples in Text

EXAMPLES:

As the <u>fruit</u> is picked, the baskets fill with <u>oranges, apples, and pears.</u>

The fishermen caught many <u>fish</u> including <u>bream, catfish, and bass.</u>

Strategies for Context Clues

Uncover the Unknown

Teach the student to use these strategies to identify a word in context.

1. Read the entire sentence without the unknown word.
2. Read the sentences or words before and after the unknown word.
3. Remove the prefix and/or suffix, then read the base or root word.
4. Find the word's meaning in the dictionary.
5. Ask a friend.
6. When everything else fails, ask the teacher.

ASSESSING AND DIAGNOSING VOCABULARY

Miscue Analysis

According to Constance Weaver (1998), "A miscue is an oral response that differs from what the text would lead us to expect." For example, a miscue occurs when the reader makes an effort to say a word but his pronunciation does not match the word's correct pronunciation. The reading error may be the result of a phonics error, inadequate sight word recognition skills, or a guess based on incorrect use of context clues.

The following guidelines to identify miscues are adapted from the work of Yetta Goodman (1998):

1. Make the reader physically and emotionally comfortable.
2. Sit beside the reader with a copy of the passage.

3. Explain the purposes for identifying miscues.

4. Tell the student to read as though he is reading to himself.

5. Model various ways to guess the pronunciation of a word.

6. Ask the reader if he has any questions.

7. Mark each miscue on the passage copy.

8. Remind the student to guess after 30 seconds elapses.

9. Commend the reader.

The purpose of miscue analysis is to determine the type of mistake the reader is making as he attempts to say a word. Make a note of the strategy he uses when he encounters an unknown word. Does the student use phonics to unlock initial, medial, and final consonant sounds in syllables? Is the student using phonics to unlock the vowel sounds? Make notes of the observed errors with the date. Analyze the types of errors, and look for patterns to plan strategies for correcting them. A checklist follows for use when reading for miscue analysis (Clay, 1993).

When Reading for Miscue Analysis

I. Phrasing and Fluency

A. Read: ____ Word by word ____ In short phrases
____ In longer phrases ____ Punctuation

B. Intonation: ____ Emerging ____ Developing ____ Effective

C. Reading Rate: ____ Slow ____ Inconsistent ____ Adequate
____ Too fast ____ Adjusted appropriately

II. Trouble Shooting

A. Problems
solved by: ____ Picture cues ____ Rereading ____ Letter sounds
____ Symbols ____ Pausing ____ No correction

B. Appeals
for help: ____ Often ____ Sometimes ____ Rarely ____ Not at all

C. Number
of words told
by teacher: _____

III. Analysis of Errors

    A. Self-corrected miscues that   ____ Did not make sense
                                              ____ Did not sound right
                                              ____ Did not look right

    B. Miscues interfered
       with meaning: ____ Yes ____ Sometimes ____ No

IV. Initial Retelling Including

    A. Tell the passage in your own words.
       ___ Character __ Setting ___ Important details
       ___ Vocabulary or phrases from reading
       ___ Events in sequence ____ Events out of sequence ___ Ending

    B. When asked to tell me more:
       Added more information about
       ___Character ___Events ___Settings ___Important details ___Endings

V. Follow-Up Questions

    A. Did you like what you read? ___ Yes ___ No Why? Why not?
    B. What does this story make you think of?

What to Do with a Miscue

The following miscues have several possible solutions. Each activity engages the reader. Use the student's favorite "ways of learning" to teach him how to correct his mistakes while reading content information.

Letter Sound Recognition Errors

- Write the letters in sand, pudding, shaving cream, or lotion.
- Use shoestrings to match uppercase letters and lowercase letters.
- Create the letters with pipe cleaners, dough, licorice, and yarn.
- Practice the letters on a magic slate, a gel bag, a blackboard, or a transparency.
- Identify the letters in alphabet cereal, advertisements, and the names of classmates.
- Participate with board games and puzzles requiring letter recognition.
- Play a challenging game such as a scavenger hunt.
- Race to find letters in easy books, newspapers, magazines, telephone books, and television guides.

Insertions

- Read easy books.
- Play games with sight words.
- Allow student to read orally with the teacher.
- Record the reading and replay it as the student follows the words.
- Praise the reader when he reads a sentence without insertions.

Omissions

- Use reminders to slow down to pay attention to individual words.
- Use a pen light or highlighter to underline words as they are read.
- Record the student as he reads and ask him to follow the words as he listens.
- Use choral or partner reading.
- Ignore it, if the meaning is not changed and it is not a habit.

Substitutions

- Emphasize the use of initial consonant sounds.
- Read easy books.
- Use the Follow the Leader strategy.
- Read with recorded books.
- Praise the reader when he completes a passage without substitutions.

Reversals

- Color-code the first and last letters in the word, using one color for the first letter and one color for the last letter.
- Color-code the right and left side of the desk, using the same colors chosen for the first and last letter in a word.
- Color-code left and right hands.
- Use a piece of cardboard, index card, or strip of paper as a guide under each sentence.
- Use a word processing program to practice typing the word.

Repetitions

- Check word attack skills.
- Have the student read the passage silently before reading it orally.
- Encourage the student to develop awareness of the repetition.
- Help build sight word skills.
- Arrange for student to read with books on CD or on tape.
- Use choral reading.

Master Multiple Meaning

Be aware of words with specific meanings in the subject that students may confuse with a common use of the words. When learning words in a particular subject, the student naturally relates the meaning to his prior knowledge and connotations. For example, the word *root* appears in the study of plants. It is confusing when the student begins a study of "square roots" in a math class. Consider the tricky or confusing words with multiple meanings in the following list:

Root

The plant's <u>root</u> grew beside the underground rock.

The square <u>root</u> of nine is three.

Our neighbor yelled when she saw the pig <u>root</u> in her flower garden.

It may take time to find the <u>root</u> of your problem.

Note: The words *root* and *route* can be confusing too.

Line

The teacher drew a <u>line</u> drawn under the word.

We stood in <u>line</u> for concert tickets.

The fishing <u>line</u> broke when he caught the large catfish.

Did you follow his <u>line</u> of thinking?

What is your <u>line</u> of work?

Create a time<u>line</u> of the music star's life.

Hang the shirt on the clothes<u>line</u> to dry.

The first <u>line</u> in the story was exciting.

The newspaper head<u>line</u> was about the rescue.

A <u>line</u> separates the numerator and denominator in a fraction.

The time changed when we crossed the state <u>line</u>.

Run

<u>Run</u> the motor of the car to warm the engine on a cold morning.

How many times did Abraham Lincoln <u>run</u> for public office?

We watched the cowboys <u>run</u> the cattle across the prairie.

Have you watched clear water <u>run</u> over rocks in a creek?

Did you <u>run</u> up a bill during the long distance call?

His mom asks him to <u>run</u> the vacuum cleaner each Saturday.

We need to <u>run</u> a set of papers for the next class.

Mastered Words: Check It Out!

The student masters a word when he reads and uses it accurately and automatically. Assess a student's mastered sight words with a word list. Ask the student to read words out of context for an accurate count of his sight word ability. When a student reads from a list, he does not have context clues or other cues to use in recalling the words. He pronounces the words in isolation.

This assessment activity checks the student's word recall. Words selected are from the pupil's unit of study or a leveled vocabulary list. Scoring includes recording responses to the following questions:

1. Is he reading the word with instant recall?   Yes   No   (Tally)
2. Is the word correctly pronounced?   Yes   No   (Tally)
3. How much is the student struggling with the word list?
   Discomfort ◄————————► Comfort
4. Does the student sound out the words on the list?
   Yes   Attempted   No
5. Does the student read the list without hesitation?
   Yes   Sometimes   No
6. Others _____

Teacher-Made Vocabulary Checklists

Create a teacher-made vocabulary checklist. Use essential vocabulary words from topics in the content area. Include words needed for the reader's success. This checklist is an effective tool to assess the reader's word knowledge base before, during, and after the learning.

Informal Reading Inventories (IRI) for Vocabulary

Informal Reading Inventories (IRIs) are vocabulary assessments designed to determine a student's reading level. The inventories identify his ability level with sight words, oral reading, and comprehension.

Graded word lists and reading passages are used. The word lists and passages usually include all grade levels from pre-primer to the eighth

Figure 4.6 Variations

Summarize.	Draw conclusions.	Retell.
Relate to today's world.	List facts.	Write passage in own words.
Relate to self.	Evaluate author's purpose.	Develop a critique for a magazine

grade. The most effective IRIs are created by the teacher to meet the diverse needs of the readers in his own classroom, but the IRI is available for purchase.

Use the following guidelines to develop an IRI to identify a student's vocabulary level:

1. Use graded word lists.

2. Choose an easy word list for the student to read.

3. Record the student's errors so that appropriate skills and strategies can be used in future lesson plans.

4. If the student reads all words on the list or misses one word, ask him to read the words on the next level.

5. Stop when the student misses two words on a list.

6. Record the list's grade level.

7. Provide reading materials on the grade level indicated by this list.

When using the IRI process, be sure to cover the following steps:

1. Introduce the passage to motivate the student to read it.

2. Ask the student to answer explicit detailed questions about the text content. These questions are designed to identify the reader's comprehension abilities.

3. Ask the student to answer questions that require implicit thinking about the passage. The learner writes a response or answers orally to demonstrate his understanding of the text beyond the surface meaning (see Figure 4.6).

Important points to remember:

- Use content text. This demonstrates how the student approaches reading assignments.

- Use high-interest material. Higher comprehension occurs when the student has a high interest in the material.
- Look through the passage for difficult vocabulary words. Choose wisely.

CLOZE PROCESS

The Cloze Reading Assessment checks the student's use of context clues for comprehension. Cloze procedures can be used either to assess the language ability of a reader, to test mastery of concepts, to test mastery of specialized vocabulary of the topic, or to test reading ability of the text.

In the cloze process, the teacher rewrites a content passage with every tenth word omitted. The reader uses content background, his prior knowledge, and his thinking skills to fill in the blanks with the word that completes the meaning correctly. Variations for differentiation include leaving out fewer words or leaving out content vocabulary or concept words.

SUMMARY

Introduce new vocabulary words related to the current topic of study. It is not easy for a student to remember words in isolation, so create meaningful connections. Mnemonic devices and novelty place a word in long-term memory, so model gimmicks and tricks the student can use to remember words. Show him how to create mnemonics and use innovative strategies. Orchestrate experiences with each new vocabulary word using stimulating, unique, and meaningful strategies, so the learner's mind takes ownership of the word.

Strategically plan differentiated vocabulary instruction with lessons and assignments so that each student's quests to learn new words become intriguing challenges for a lifetime. Use the following poem to illustrate that vocabulary acquisition is a valuable lifetime quest.

Better Than Money in the Bank
In rhymes, menus, movies,
And raps you see them there.
When you learn new vocabulary words
You can use them easily everywhere.
When you master a new word
And use it with ease in the right place
It is stored in your vocabulary bank
Until you say it or write it in the right space.
Vocabulary words can make
Others think you are very, very smart.
You can use them in important speeches
Or write one to touch a good friend's heart.

—Chapman and King, 2003

The Art of Decoding 5

Decoding is an essential skill that readers use to understand unknown words. *Decoding* a word includes dividing the word into syllables, applying the rules of phonics, and identifying the root or base word. The art of applying decoding skills lets the reader put all the articulate bits together to produce the word's sounds. Most students need to know the art of decoding to become a fluent reader. Teachers must know the rules to be able to infuse them into content lessons, because students encounter words that follow the rules (and some that are exceptions to the rules) in their vocabulary lessons or when reading assignments in any subject area.

If the science lesson introduces the word *equator* or the math lesson introduces the word *numerator*, this is the time to teach the controlling *r* rule. When the rule is integrated across the curriculum, the student sees the validity of learning this rule. Plan and implement systematic, explicit phonics instruction and decoding skills if the student does not have the background knowledge to be able to apply the rules of phonics.

PHONICS INSTRUCTION

Phonics skill instruction provides a foundation the student can draw upon to recognize and pronounce letter sounds and their combinations when he sees them in print. Students who master letter–sound correspondence have a tool to help them read more accurately and fluently. Some students struggle to decode words because they have little knowledge or understanding of letter–sound relationships. The application of phonics rules guides many readers of all ages to recognize and pronounce words.

No other aspect of the language arts curriculum has received as much attention as phonics. There are two sides to this issue (Bauman, Hoffman, Moon, & Duffy-Hester, 1998). One school of thought is that phonetic skills are most effective when taught in isolation in a quality reading program.

Others think a sight vocabulary develops through literature-based programs.

Phonics instruction usually receives more emphasis in lower grades than in upper grades, but phonics instruction offered in the upper grades benefits students who did not develop phonetic awareness in the early grades (Pressley, 1998). Also, some students simply need a phonics review. Some need to develop a basic knowledge base of letter sounds. Many learners know the rules but cannot apply them as they encounter them in reading. Most students need a strong phonics program to build independent word attack skills. It is essential for the reader to apply phonics and use analysis skills to decode words. The use of innovative, varied activities and active student participation can teach a reader of any age how to remember and apply the rules.

The art of decoding may be the missing link a student needs to become a successful reader.

THE PHONICS DOZEN (THE FONIX DUZEN!)

The following section describes a dozen phonics skills a reader should know and be able to apply. Use the activities to teach these important skills with vocabulary development and reading experiences.

Remember, a learner's speaking vocabulary is much larger than his reading vocabulary. When a student sounds out a word and hears himself saying it, the word is becoming part of his self-talk. This self-talk stimulates his thinking of past associations and experiences with the word. These mental connections give meaning to the word.

Actively engage the learner as he learns phonics rules and generalizations to pronounce words. The Phonics Dozen list contains strategies and activities to teach readers new ways to apply and remember the rules. If the reader knows how to divide words into syllables, knows the letter sounds in each syllable and the exceptions to the phonics rules, he is able to read most of the words he encounters. Think of key words and examples from the subject's vocabulary words that can be used to apply these strategies. Add to the suggestions. The sequence of steps presented here in the Phonics Dozen is an effective way to teach the skills.

Skill 1: Understand That Letters Are Symbols for Sounds That Form Words

Phonics is our alphabet's language. It is the study of *phonemes,* commonly called the "small units" or letter sounds (Griffith & Olson, 1992). Each letter has one or more distinct sounds. Often the letters combine to create blends, digraphs, or diphthongs.

The letters take their special places within an arrangement to form words. The reader uses the sounds of the letters to pronounce and recognize words.

When using phonics skills effectively, the student is able to distinguish the sounds of the letters and combine them for reading, writing, and speaking. He blends or combines sounds to decode a word. Mastered letter sounds are in the student's memory for automatic use. When mastery occurs, the learner has tools he can use to read and write words.

Alphabet Animals

Students need strategies to help them remember letter sounds. The initial consonant and vowel sounds in the Alphabet Animal lines provide key words the reader can use to recall letter sounds. Use one line to introduce each sound as needs. Use a chanting rhythm or the tune "Are You Sleeping?" to teach the letter sounds as shown in the following example:

> Short *a* says /a/. Short *a* says /a/.
> /a/ as in Andy. /a/ as in Andy.
> Andy Ant acts anxious. Andy Ant acts anxious.
> /a/, /a/, /a/— /a/, /a/, /a/. (repeating the short *a* sound)

Amos Ape ate apricots.	Andy Ant acts anxious.
Bobby Bee buys big bikes.	Cathy Cow catches colds.
Cindy Centipede circles cities.	Dottie Dog digs deep ditches.
Eva Emu eats éclairs.	Ed Elephant edits essays.
Felicia Fish found four fans.	Goofy Goat gets goggles.
George Giraffe gips gerbils.	Henry Horse hauls heavy hay.
Irene Ibis ices icicles.	Inky Inchworm inhales insects.
Jeffrey Jaguar juggles jars.	Kate Kangaroo kisses kings.
Lucy Lion licks lollipops.	Mandy Monkey makes music.
Nancy Newt needs nice news.	Oscar Ostrich offers options.
Opal Opossum opened oatmeal.	Paula Parrot paints purple pigs.
Queenie Quail quits quickly.	Rosie Rabbit races roosters.
Silly Seal sings silly songs.	Tony Turtle tells tall tales.
Uly Unicorn uses unicycles.	Uncle Ugly unhooks umbrellas.
Victor Vulture visits Vermont.	Willie Wolf wears watches.

Extra X X-rays X's.   Yetta Yak yanks yoyos.

Zeke Zebra zips zippers.

Skill 2: Identify the Consonants

Rule A: The consonants constitute all the letters of the alphabet except for the vowels. The vowels are *a, e, i, o, u,* and sometimes *w* and *y.*

Rule B: When the same two consonants are side by side in the same syllable, only one of the two consonant sounds is heard.

Examples: ha<u>ll</u>way   gra<u>ss</u>   mi<u>tt</u>

Skill 3: Recognize That Hard and Soft Consonants Make Different Sounds

Rule A: The letter *c* makes a hard and a soft sound.

1. The letter *c* makes the hard /k/ sound before *a, o,* and *u.*

    Examples: castle copper custom

2. The letter *c* makes the soft /s/ sound before *e, i,* and *y.*

    Examples: cell cider cycle

Try the following technique to teach the reader how to distinguish between the hard and soft consonant sounds: Place a hand over the throat while pronouncing the soft sound of *c.* The vocal cords will not vibrate. Make the hard sound of *c* and feel the vibration.

Rule B: The letter *g* makes a hard and a soft sound.

1. The letter *g* makes the hard sound before *a, o,* and *u.*

    Examples: gangster gorilla guppy

2. The letter *g* makes the soft sound before *e, i,* and *y.*

    Examples: genius gigantic gym

Try the vocal cord test to distinguish between the hard and soft *g* sounds.

Goofy Collage

1. Divide a sheet of paper in half.

2. Cut out pictures and words that have a hard *c* and *g* sound anywhere in the word.

3. In a graffiti way, do the following:

   - Paste the words and pictures with the hard *c* sound on the top half of the paper.
   - Paste the words and pictures with the hard *g* sound on the bottom half of the paper.

Variation. Repeat the activity for the soft *c* and *g* sounds.

Camouflaged Consonants: A Poem

> *c* and *g* are tricky consonants, you see.
> They don't say what you expect them to be.
> Some vowels change the way *c* and *g* sound.
> It depends on the vowel hanging around.
> *c* and *g* will change the sounds they make.
> Three vowels soften the noise they create.
> If *e, i,* or *y* comes after the *c*
> *c* makes the /s/ sound easily.
> Listen to soft *c*'s whistle and whisper.
> As you say *center, cyclone,* and *cinder.*
> If *e, i,* or *y* comes after *g,*
> *g* makes the /j/ sound easily.
> *g* makes the soft /j/ sound to trick you and me.
> Say *giraffe, gelatin, gentle,* and *gypsy.*

Sounds of c and g Chart

Post the following chart for reference as students work with the *c* and *g* sounds. Use a dark, vibrant color as the background for the hard sounds. Use a soft pastel color as a background for the soft sounds.

	a o u	e i y
	Hard Sounds	*Soft Sounds*
c	cat cold cut	cease city cyclone
g	gap go gum	genius giraffe gym

Rule C: The letter *s* often makes the sound of /z/ at the end of a syllable. Examples: families enemies cookies please babies rose

Activity: S in Disguise

1. Brainstorm a list of words in which the letter *s* disguises himself as he makes the /z/ sound.

2. In small groups or with partners, play charades with words that follow this rule.

3. Post a class list of words that show *S* in Disguise.

Skill 4: Recognize Consonant Blends

Rule: Two or more consonants using their sounds together are *blends.* Each letter sound is heard as the blend is pronounced. Blends that occur at the beginnings of words are called *initial blends.* Blends that occur at the ends of words are called *final blends.* Blends are also referred to as *consonant clusters.*

Examples of Initial Consonant Blends

bl	cl	fl	gl	pl	sl	br	cr	
dr	fr	gr	pr	sc	scr	sk	sl	sm
sn	sp	spr	st	str	sw	thr	tr	tw

Examples of Final Consonant Blends

ft	nd	st	ld	lk	mp

Try This Rhyme: Blend Friends

> If two or three consonants blend their sounds together,
> You hear the sound of each and every letter.
> Blends are in words at the beginning, middle, or end.
> Say *spook, plant, publish, skate, sport,* and *friend.*

Activity: Blend Blast

1. Scan the topic content to find key words that begin with blends.

2. Create a list of the words, and sort the words that have the same blends.

3. Define *blend alliteration* for the students and share some examples. Alliterations are words that have the same beginning sounds.

   Examples:

   - Fresh frozen fruit freezes freaky friends.
   - Dreaming dragons draw dreadfully.
   - Strange straggling strangers stroll straight streets.

4. Ask the students to use words from the list to create alliterations and illustrate them.

5. Share and celebrate.

6. Design an alliteration bulletin board, mobile, or T-shirt.

Skill 5: Use the Sounds of Consonant Digraphs

Rule: When two consonant letters make one sound, they form a *consonant digraph*.

The following is a list of consonant digraphs with their sounds and some word examples.

ch /ch/	chain	champ	chart	cheese
ch /k/	character	chemical	chorus	chrome
ch /sh/	chef	chalet	charade	chandelier
gh /g/	ghetto	ghost	ghastly	ghoul
gh /f/	cough	enough	laugh	tough
ph /f/	phase	phone	phonics	elephant
sh /sh/	shade	fish	shark	shawl
wh	whack	wheat	wheel	whine

(voiced)

th /th/	than	that	the	those

(voiceless)

th /th/	thaw	theater	third	thumb

Consonant digraphs with silent letters:

gn /n/	align	gnarl	gnash	gnaw
kn /n/	knack	knee	knife	knock
wr /r/	wrangler	wrap	wrestle	wrist
ck /k/	chicken	clock	flick	shock
tch /ch/	batch	catch	latch	match
dge /j/	badge	dodge	fudge	grudge

Activity 1: Digging Digraphs

1. Create sentences from words using the same digraph to form alliterations.

2. Illustrate the alliterations.

Examples:

Shiny sharks shake shimmering shells.

Whimpering whales whine while whistling.

Activity 2: Digraph Dash

1. Take your text, paper, and pencil and meet with a partner.

2. Set a timer for 2 or 3 minutes.

3. Individually dash through the text to find words that contain digraphs.

4. Write the word and the page number on a list.

5. Exchange lists and check to see that all words contain digraphs.

6. When the Digraph Dash ends, count the number of words on the list.

7. Celebrate with the winner.

8. Repeat the game but reduce the time limit. Try to increase the number of words on the list in each Digraph Dash.

Skill 6: Recognize Long Vowel Sounds

A *long vowel* says its name as it is heard when the alphabet is stated. Remember, the vowels are *a, e, i, o, u,* and sometimes *w* and *y*.

Long vowel sounds are heard in these words: pl<u>ay</u> b<u>ea</u>d   <u>i</u>ce   c<u>oa</u>t   m<u>u</u>le   sk<u>y</u>

Note: The letters *w* and *y* may have double duty because they can act as vowels or consonants. For this reason they are often referred to as *semivowels*.

Rule A: When a word or syllable has a vowel on the end, the vowel usually has a long sound.

> If a single vowel is on the end of a syllable that you see
> He says his alphabet name because he feels fancy free.

Examples:

<u>ba</u>by   b<u>e</u>   tr<u>i</u>cycle   s<u>o</u>   m<u>u</u>sic   sk<u>y</u>

Rule B: When two vowels are together, the first one is usually long and the second one is silent.

> Strange things happen when two vowels in a syllable meet.
> The first one is usually long; the second one is asleep.

Figure 5.1   Long vowel key for football

a	e	i	o	u
game chain	tee team	line hike	go goal	rule uniform

Examples:

stream   raid   beat   goat   dye

Rule C: When a word or syllable has a silent *e* on the end, the first vowel is long.

Use the vowel key in Figure 5.1 as a guide for students to recall vowel sounds. Each word in this example relates to football, but the teacher can create a key chart or poster using vocabulary words in the topic or an area of interest.

Skill 7: Apply the Rules for the Final e

Rule: If a word or syllable has two vowels, and the second vowel is a final *e*, usually the first vowel is long and the final *e* is silent.

> When a syllable has a vowel, a consonant, and ends in the letter *e*
> The first vowel is long; the letter *e* is as silent as it can be.

Examples:

brave   bone   smile   assume   scheme   style

Skill 8: Recognize That Short Vowels Make Their Own Sounds

Rule: When there is a vowel at the beginning or middle of a syllable followed by a consonant, the vowel is usually short. The vowels are *a, e, i, o, u,* and sometimes *y* and *w*. Short vowels also include ∂ (schwa), which is pronounced "uh," and is the shortest vowel of them all (example: circus).

You hear the short vowel sounds in: bat bed mitt socks luck

Short Vowel Key for Football

a	e	i	o	u
pass	end	kick	block	run

Figure 5.2   Vowel play

	A	E	I	O	U
Long					
Short					
Controlling R					

Scared Short

When a syllable has a vowel between consonants without a
vowel friend,
He uses his short sound just to hide and pretend.
Listen as you say *tap, kit, hop, fin, fat, cut, sit,* and *win*
Now say each of the words with a silent *e* on the end.

Assessment of Vowel Sounds

Ask students to fill in the grid in Figure 5.2 with a word that is an
example of the vowel rule.

Skill 9: Know the Sounds of Phonograms

A *phonogram* begins with a vowel. It is a combination of letters that
ends a word or syllable. Examples:

ab	an	eal	ent	int	oar	ort	up
ack	and	eat	er	ip	oat	oss	ug
ad	ang	eed	ice	iss	on	ote	ule
ag	ank	eel	ick	it	one	ound	ull
ail	ap	eep	id	ite	ond	ong	um
ain	at	eet	im	ine	ook	ump	ut
ait	ate	eg	in	ing	ool	un	ute
ake	am	elf	ine	ink	oom	ung	
all	an	en	ind	int	oon	unk	
ame	ead	end	ing	oat	ore	unt	

Go for It!

1. Make a center, word, or bulletin board for rhyming words using these phonograms.

2. Challenge the student to list as many rhyming words as possible.

3. Provide the materials for the student to create games and activities with rhyming words.

Recognize Vowel Digraphs

Digraphs are two vowel letters that make one sound.

Examples:

short oo	foot	shook
long oo	shoot	tooth
au	haul	caught
aw	squawk	crawl
ew	few	nephew

Skill 10: Recognize Vowel Diphthongs

Rule: Two or more vowels blending their sounds together form a *diphthong*. Each letter sound is heard when the diphthong is pronounced.
The most common diphthongs are *oy, oi, ow,* and *ou.*

Sentence Challenge

Challenge students to make up sentences using words with the diphthongs.
Example: The boy spoiled Roy's proud cow.

Diphthong Glide

> Most vowels are short, silent, or long,
> But some get together and form a diphthong.
> When two vowels join together side by side
> They often make a new sound as they glide.
> *Oink, towel, grouch, spoil, ouch,* and *ground*
> All are words with a diphthong sound.
> *w* and *y* become vowels like they're wearing a disguise.
> Say *growl, toy, wow,* and *boy* to be diphthong wise.

Skill 11: Make the Sounds of the Vowels When the Controlling r Follows the Vowel

Rule: The letter *r* controls vowels. The vowel sound before the letter *r* is neither long nor short. It has a new, unique sound.

Examples:

ar	cartoon	partner	yard
er	jersey	mermaid	servant
ir	birth	first	giraffe
or	dorm	normal	score
ur	survive	blur	curtain

The Consonant R in Command

> The letter *r* takes complete vowel control.
> He makes vowels take a unique sound in their new role.
> Watch *r* command change in vowel sounds everywhere.
> Listen to the words *star, germ, chirp, work, turn*, and *there*.

Skill 12: Use the Proper Sounds of *y*

Rule A: When the letter *y* is at the end of a one-syllable word that contains no other vowel, the *y* usually makes the long *i* sound.

Examples:

sky   shy   fly

Rule B: If the letter *y* is the last letter of a syllable with no other vowels, it usually makes the sound of long *e* or long *i*.

Examples:

baby   century   satisfy   terrify   terribly

STRUCTURAL ANALYSIS

Structural analysis identifies words by dividing and examining their parts. Word analysis uses root words, word origins, prefixes, suffixes, and syllables. The reader uses these keys to decode, attack, and pronounce an unknown word.

Figure 5.3 Common roots

Root	Origin	Meaning	Words
cap	Latin	head	captain, capital
ced	Latin	believe	credit, creditor
cycl	Greek	circle	bicycle, tricycle
deci	Greek	ten	decimeter, decimal
dyna	Greek	power	dynamite, dynamic
geo	Greek	geo	geography, geometry
gon	Greek	angle	polygon, hexagon
ped	Latin	foot	pedal, pediatrician
phon	Greek	sound	phonics, telephone
scribe	Latin	write	describe, subscribe
vid	Latin	see	video, evident

Root Words

Our language includes various forms of words. Root words change their meaning when prefixes and suffixes are added to them. A student needs to know how to divide a word into syllables using root words and affixes.

A *root word* is the origin of a word family (see Figure 5.3). A root word often is referred to as the *base* or *stem*. The spelling of a root word often changes when a suffix is added (as in *merry/merrily*).

Prefixes

A *prefix* attaches to the beginning of a word (see Figure 5.4). It changes the meaning of the word. It is easy to remember the meaning of the word *prefix*: *pre* means "before" and *fix* means "to place," so a prefix is placed before the root word. Think about *dislike, rework, unpack, precede*, and *preview*.

Content-Related Prefixes

Most subject areas have prefixes that are used with vocabulary words related to the topic studied. Identify these prefixes and teach them while introducing the topic. Make the list and post it!

Figure 5.4 Common prefixes

Prefix	Meaning	Words
ad	to	adapt, addict, admit
auto	self	automobile, automatic, autobiography
co	together	coauthor, cooperate, coexistence
dis	opposite	discharge, displeasure, distrustful
en	put in to	enclose, endanger, enrollment
extra	outside	extraordinary, extraterrestrial, extrasensory
for/fore	first part	foresight, forefather, foreclose
il	not	illegal, illiterate, illogical
im	into	immerse, implant, import
im	not	immature, imperfect, imprison
in	not	inability, incomplete, inhumane
inter	across	international, interview, interweave
mis	wrong	misfortune, misfit, misspent
non	not	nonsense, nonstop, nonresident
re	again	rebuilt, reforest, reprint
re	back	recall, repay, retract
trans	across	transportation, transoceanic, transatlantic
un	not	unattractive, unclasp, unorganized

Math Examples:

bi   co   contra   equi   kilo   mono   multi

octa   peri   quad   rect   semi   tri

Suffixes

A *suffix* is a syllable with a special meaning that is added to the end of a word (see Figure 5.5). Often the ending completely changes the meaning of the word.

Figure 5.5 Common suffixes

Suffix	Meaning	Words
ade	action	blockade, escapade, stockade
ant	one who	assistant, merchant, servant
cle	small	cubicle, particle, article
ic	relating to	comic, historic, mimic
let	small	booklet, leaflet, starlet
ly	similar to	motherly, sickly, worldly
or	one who	actor, doctor, donor

Syllables

Introducing Syllables!

Syllables divide words into small parts. Each syllable contains one vowel sound. The vowel sound and its consonants create the syllable. There are as many syllables in a word as there are vowel sounds. Demonstrate how to pronounce the small parts or syllables in words and put them together to pronounce larger words.

Syllable Rules

Rule 1: When two consonants come between two vowels, the word is usually divided between the consonants.

Examples: ex/tend   man/ners   yel/low   fun/gus

Rule 2: When one consonant comes between two vowels, divide the word after the first vowel.

Examples: re/turn   ro/tate   pre/view   pro/fessional

Rule 3: If a word ends in a consonant that is followed by the letters *le*, the consonant and *le* will form the last syllable.

Examples: bub/ble   bicy/cle   nib/ble   gam/ble

Rule 4: Divide a word after a prefix.

Examples: re/construct   sub/marine   bi/cycle   trans/portation

Rule 5: Divide a word before the suffix.

Examples: teach/er   eleva/tion   tempera/ment   quick/ly

Syllable Stand-Off!

1. Assign partners or small groups.

2. Use the text to find high-challenge words with three or more syllables.

3. Students apply the syllable rules to the content vocabulary words.

4. Post the rules on card headings around the room.

5. Students place their words under the rule that divides the syllables. Keep adding words to form a word wall for reference.

Syllable Sense

> Syllables show you how to say a new word.
> Each part is said with sounds you've heard.
> In every syllable, in every word,
> At least one vowel sound is heard.
> Clap each part of a word you know.
> Each clap counts a syllable as you go.
> You can count syllables with your chin
> Your chin drops to signal a syllable's end.
> Count the syllables this new way
> So you'll know little word parts to say.

Syllable Riddles

Create a riddle using a word that has multiple syllables.

Example:

> I have four feet.
> I hang by my tail.
> I have two syllables.
> What am I? (Monkey)

Accent Rules and Clues

If you can pronounce the word, you can figure out which syllable is accented. Say the word in a phrase or in a sentence quickly, and listen to which syllable has the most emphasis. That is the accented or stressed syllable.

Figure 5.6   The Phonics Dozen Checklist. Use this checklist to assess the weaknesses and strengths of a student's phonics use. Use it periodically to monitor the progress of a student as he grows in his decoding ability.

Student's Name _____   Class/Subject _____

Observation Dates   A. 1st Date _____   Observer _____

                      B. 2nd Date _____   Observer _____

                      C. 3rd Date _____   Observer _____

The student is able to

     A   B   C

1. ☐   ☐   ☐   Understand that letters are symbols for sounds that form words

2. ☐   ☐   ☐   Identify the consonants

3. ☐   ☐   ☐   Understand that hard and soft consonants make different sounds

4. ☐   ☐   ☐   Recognize consonant blends

5. ☐   ☐   ☐   Use the sounds of the consonant digraphs

6. ☐   ☐   ☐   Use the long and short vowel sounds

7. ☐   ☐   ☐   Apply the rules for final e

8. ☐   ☐   ☐   Understand that short vowels make their own sounds

9. ☐   ☐   ☐   Know the common phonograms

10. ☐   ☐   ☐   Recognize the vowel diphthongs

11. ☐   ☐   ☐   Make the sounds of the vowels when the controlling r follows the vowels

12. ☐   ☐   ☐   Use the proper sounds of y

Comments A	Comments B	Comments C

There are rules to decide where the stress is placed. Stressed syllables help to pronounce and recognize unknown multi-syllable words.

Rule 1. Prefixes and suffixes are usually not accented.

un COV er   un FRIEND ly

Rule 2. First syllables are usually accented in base or root words with no prefixes or suffixes.

A pril   PEN cil

Rule 3. The meaning changes in some words by a shift in accent.

CON tent   con TENT

OB ject   ob JECT

SUMMARY

Teachers' strategies for infusing phonics in their everyday planning must be assessed and adjusted daily to meet the needs of the diverse learners in their classrooms (see Figure 5.6).

Students need to be introduced to the word *phonics* and to realize the value of knowing how to sound out words phonetically. The teaching of the phonics skills and rules works best and most effectively if it happens when the students need the information and if the students learn to apply the skills and rules in their vocabulary words introduced in the units and topics of study. This is embedding phonics instruction in the act of reading and can be used during the reading and writing of the word. So remember to identify words and letters in the text and in the print-rich environment. This shows the value of phonics in everyday use and application.

Observe, assess, and evaluate students closely while they are reading and writing to identify their individual needs. Remove the fear of sounding out words! Present strategies for structural analysis as meaningful activities instead of dreaded events. Using this approach, difficult words become inviting challenges because the teacher supplied the reader with tools he can easily apply in the art of decoding.

Comprehension

6

Reading comprehension skills are critical to the student's success with texts and related materials in all subject areas. Each student has the right to become a comprehending reader. Differentiate instructional strategies for reading comprehension to meet the diverse needs of readers.

> When I understand what a word means
> I can use it to understand scenes.
> When I do not know what the words say
> I unlock the meaning in my own way.
> When I do not understand.
> I search for clues close at hand.

> —Chapman and King, 2003

WHY DIFFERENTIATE COMPREHENSION STRATEGIES?

The Reader's Background Knowledge Varies on Each Topic

Each reader in the classroom knows different amounts of information about the topic. This knowledge base is a result of past experiences. Learning builds from one experience to the next. In the introduction of a lesson, the learner makes links with his prior knowledge. He may think, "Oh, I remember that!" or, "We learned something about this last year." During the learning, the student applies these links. Readers need to learn how to consciously connect to their background knowledge. After the reading, the learner links to his world, develops emotional ties, identifies interests for further exploration, and concludes how he is going to use the new information learned.

Interest Levels Vary with Each Learner

Challenge and motivate the reader using his areas of interests and strengths to provide successful, pleasant learning experiences. Develop assignments as opportunities that lead the student to explore and discover more about a topic in his area of interest. The student's interest level affects his attitude toward reading a selection. For instance, one reader may feel that he will be successful with an assignment. Another student may exhibit a negative attitude that is a result of his feeling of failure as he turns to the first page to begin reading.

Each Student's Ability to Read the Materials Differs

Each reader varies in his ability to read the material. He may be able to read the materials but not be able to tell about the information read. Another student may not be able to read the words because of his inability to decode words or because he has a limited sight word vocabulary in this topic. A student may be aware of the rule but lack the ability to apply it. Another student may understand the rule and be able to use it automatically as needed to understand information. The mastery level of each reader's comprehension skills and strategies is unique.

Students Use Different Approaches to Understand Information They Are Reading

A reader usually has a preference for how he comprehends reading materials. A reader may comprehend best when he reads the information aloud. One student may understand the information when he reads silently. Another student may need to hear the information read aloud.

Many times the reader goes through the motions of the learning with the teacher. The information is taught, but the student does not remember it. Effective learning occurs when the student sees a need for the information and retains it as his own to use and apply to other situations. The power of teaching is creating this "buy-in" for the learner.

BARRIERS TO COMPREHENSION

One cause of poor comprehension is inappropriate background knowledge or experience with the topic information. A student who has little exposure to the topic is prone to have less ability to adapt the new information and skills than will a student who is more experienced in the topic.

The reader may be reading in a place or position that hinders his comprehension. He needs to be in a comfortable place where he can concentrate without distractions or interruptions.

Inadequate sight word recognition, word attack skills, and vocabulary knowledge are barriers to understanding. Often a student learns a skill or strategy just for the moment. He is unable to remember or recall comprehension skills that he once learned. He applies the skill in an immediate situation, but he is unable to apply the same skill later. If a student does not recall facts and details in a selection, he may have no interest in the assigned topic. This unmotivated, "turned off' reader is bored with the information.

Emotional barriers also influence comprehension ability. For example, if a student believes he cannot read, his feelings interfere with his ability to comprehend. The reader's "I can't" attitude is a barrier to comprehension. He must believe he can read the material and understand it using the comprehension tools in his repertoire. The "I can't" attitude must be changed to the "I can," because the reader's attitude affects his altitude or level of success with comprehension skills. In the words of Robert Sylwester, "Our emotional system drives our attentional system, which drives learning and memory and everything else that we do. It is biologically impossible to learn and remember anything that we don't pay attention to" (interview with Marcia D'arcangelo, 1998).

From Isolation to Connection

Many students learn skills for immediate use or for the next test. Brain research proves that an individual learns when he needs the information. When the reader feels that he needs to know the information in a passage, he has a desire to read and understand.

Teachers build new learning on prior knowledge. When there is an effective link between prior knowledge and new learning, the new knowledge is easier to learn, remember, and retrieve. Teaching isolated facts is not as effective as newer evidence-based approaches that teach for understanding and a higher rate of transfer of knowledge to long-term memory (see Figure 6.1).

Figure 6.1 Comparison of yesterday's and today's reading instruction

Teaching Isolated Facts	Teaching for Understanding
• Material or facts covered	• Materials or facts processed
• Fragmented skills	• Skills link to prior knowledge
• Few links between subjects	• Many links to other subjects
• Low level thinking	• All levels of thinking
• Few personal connections	• Strong relations to the student's life
• Rote memory emphasized	• Long-term memory emphasized
• Learning for the moment	• High transfer of knowledge

LEVELS OF COMPREHENSION

Teachers analyze texts and create lessons based on the type of thinking students need to comprehend. The terms *online, between the lines,* and *beyond the lines* assist students in their understanding of the three levels of comprehension. Use the following levels when selecting reading materials and developing questions.

Online: Literal

Literal comprehension means the reader identifies explicitly stated main ideas, details, sequence, cause and effect relationships, and patterns. An effective reader recognizes the main ideas presented in the text as well as the supporting details. Use explicit questions and statements to discover the learner's understanding of the facts and details in a passage. Examples:

- What is the capital of Georgia?
- List the events that occurred.
- What does this word mean in this passage?

Between the Lines: Inferential Comprehension

Inferences are ideas the author shares through descriptive language. The reader derives meaning from information the author provides. The student cannot find the answer unless he understands the material. In other words, he is not able to physically point to the answer of an inferential question. Inferential reading determines main ideas, details, comparisons, and cause and effect relationships that are not explicitly stated.

Ask the student questions similar to the following to check inferential comprehension.

Examples:

- How did this person or writer feel?
- What do you think the next step will be?
- How does this event affect your life today?

Beyond the Lines: Evaluative Comprehension

Using evaluative comprehension, students are able to identify bias, make judgments, and use critical thinking skills. This includes the ability to draw conclusions, summarize, and predict outcomes.

Use the following questions and statement to determine a student's evaluative comprehension ability.

Examples:

- Why do you think this information is important?
- How does this major event affect you today?
- State your opinion on the topic.

STEPS TO READING A PASSAGE

Readers in every grade need a repertoire of comprehension strategies to use as they read subject materials. The following strategies and activities teach comprehension skills to use before, during, and after reading experiences. The Passage Preview, Passage View, and Passage Review take the reader through the comprehension process from the beginning of a reading experience to the end. Use these ideas to plan effective lessons in reading fiction and nonfiction material. Readers can easily adapt these strategies for everyday personal and academic use.

BEFORE READING: THE PASSAGE PREVIEW

Orchestrate the brain! The brain stores new information by connecting it to prior knowledge. The way a teacher prepares a student for reading experiences has an extraordinary impact on his comprehension. Make a link or connection to the learner's prior knowledge or previous experiences to enhance memory. Ask the reader to brainstorm the information he knows relating to the topic before the unit planning begins. These bridges and avenues from prior knowledge to new information create optimal learning experiences because the brain uses the links to store information for future use.

The purpose for reading the assignment is set in pre-reading activities. The reader understands (1) why he is reading the selection, (2) the essential questions, and (3) the information he is expected to gain from the reading. It is crucial to build the reader's inquiring mind! Ideal experiences during the pre-reading session build excitement and lead the reader's anticipation to the point that he says, "I cannot wait to read this!"

Match the Learner with the Learning

Match lessons with the student's knowledge. Incorporate the reader's interests and ideas in lesson planning. Prior to teaching each topic, ask, "Am I using the very best strategies to teach the reading skill based on the student's prior knowledge, experiences, and needs?" This task is accomplished by knowing the learner.

Figure 6.2   Reading rates

Fast Reading Rate	Careful Reading Rate
• Easy materials • Pleasure reading • Skimming for main ideas • Scanning for important details.	• Procedural directions • Technical terms • Difficult material • Fact-filled information • Instructions
Examples Novels Television schedule Telephone book	*Examples* Textbook assignments Manuals Directions for games

Choose the Reading Rate

The student needs to know how and when to set his reading rate. The reading purposes and the type of material determine how fast or slow the material is read (see Figure 6.2). An effective reader identifies the different types of materials that require various reading speeds. The reader's personal interest in the topic influences his reading rate.

Pre-assess Prior Knowledge

The next part of the introduction is assessing the student's prior knowledge to select information in a new unit to emphasize based on the learner's interests and needs. This involves finding out what the student knows and what he wants to know about the topic.

Planning for Pre-assessments

Planning for effective pre-assessments is essential. The information gained reveals the learner's knowledge base, his related interests, and how he feels about the upcoming study. Remember to pre-assess two or three weeks prior to teaching the unit, so the data collected can be used while planning for that group of students. This saves time. If plans are made before the assessment, the plans and the readers' needs may not match. Remember, design plans and use them strategically to meet the needs of specific groups of readers.

To find the students' knowledge base related to new information, use a variety of interesting and novel assessment tools. Choose effective formal or informal pre-assessment tools from the selection in Figure 6.3.

Figure 6.3 Pre-assessment tools for class reading a selection

Formal	Informal

Checklist
Journals
Brainstorming sessions
Pre-tests
Inventories
Rubrics
Conferences
Surveys
	Four Corners (see Fig. 6.4)
	Human Graphs
	Cards
	  Yes Maybe No
	  Often Sometimes Never
	  Got it! Know a little Not a clue
	
	Likert Scales
	  2 4 6 8
	
	  ⟵————⟶
	
	Discussions
	Conversations

Figure 6.4 Four Corners

I do not know much about this topic.	I know a little about this topic.
I know a great deal about this topic.	I am an expert on this topic!

Four Corners: An Informal Pre-assessment Tool

Tools similar to the following example provide quick, easy feedback. Write each statement listed on the chart on a separate, large piece of paper or sentence strip. Place each chart or strip sequentially in each corner of the classroom. Announce the topic. Tell students to move to the corner that describes or reflects their knowledge about the topic. Use this assessment tool before planning lessons to incorporate students' strengths, needs, and prior knowledge (see Figure 6.4).

Identify Essential Questions During a Passage Preview

According to Strong, Silver, Perini, and Tuculescu (2002), "Essential questions should be designed to stimulate the reader's interest by letting them work with the information in ways that create personal meaning." Essential questions are open-ended. They focus a student's attention on the topic and generate higher-order thinking. They create connections from prior learning to the new topic, generate predictions, and lead the reader through the passage. The questions provide purposes for reading, stimulate curiosity, and lead the reader's mind to search for answers. Teach students to use the following steps before reading an assignment.

Think

Tell the student to think and write about his knowledge and experiences related to the topic.
Examples:

- What do you know about our new topic?
- What have you studied that would compare to this subject?
- Have you read books or articles that relate to this information?

Write

Ask the student to write everything he knows about the topic.
Examples:

- What experiences have you had with the information?
- What have you heard about this topic at home or school?

Explore

Ask the students to explore the passage as a preview.
Examples:

- Look at pictures, graphs, and charts.
- Read the bold and italics print including the headings and subheadings.
- Study the summaries.
- Read questions at the end of the chapter, if they are available. This preview tells the reader what information to look for as he reads.
- Explore the text with skimming and scanning.

If the topic involves a tricky vocabulary word, ask the students to scan the text to find the new word and give a signal when they find it. Tell them to read one sentence before the word, the sentence containing the word, and the sentence following the word. This strategy helps the reader discover the meaning of the word through context clues. This has to be modeled, so the learner understands the "behind the scenes" thinking while using this strategy.

Predict

Challenge students to make learning predictions. Effective readers continually predict what will happen next. The prediction may be related to the next word or to the next event. The reader confirms or revises during the reading (see Figure 6.5).

Figure 6.5   Note Grid

Brainstorming Notes Facts, Predictions, and Thoughts	Notes During Reading Facts, Thoughts, and Conclusions

Examples:

- What do you think the author is going to share about the topic?
- What do you think are some similarities or differences between this topic and [a prior topic]?

Share

Allow students to share information about the topic.
Examples:

- How have you or would you use this information?
- Have you read books or articles that relate to the information?

Relate

Challenge the student to list interests or concerns related to the topic.
Example:

- What do you want to learn about this topic?

Encourage the student to explain his greatest worry or fear to remove barriers to the new learning.
Example:

- Are there passages, terms, or sections that are worrying you about the study of this topic? Why?

Brainstorming

A brainstorming session brings the reader's inside thinking outside. The teacher's role is to create a classroom atmosphere where each participant feels free to respond.

Brainstorming Guidelines

1. Collect and accept all ideas.
2. Avoid comments that judge, evaluate, or analyze thoughts.
3. Encourage individuals to piggyback on the ideas of others.
4. Post thoughts on a chart or board for future reference during the study. Label this "Our Brainstorming."
5. Praise and encourage all students to participate.

Brainstorming Activity

Step 1. Individual Brainstorming

Step 2. Partner or Small Group Brainstorming

a. Form partners or small groups.
b. Share individual lists from the brainstorming.
c. Ask each pair or group to discuss and compile a list of their ideas.

Step 3. Total Class Brainstorming

a. Call on each group to share the compiled list.
b. Post each key point on a chart, board, or overhead to create a class list.

Note: Use this list to make Adjustable Assignments in planning.

Grab the Reader's Attention

A *hook* is a gimmick or activity that triggers curiosity and motivates and intrigues the students to want to experience learning. Use this strategy in the introduction of a lesson to build anticipation and excitement. A special reading, a prop, a part of a music selection, a challenging puzzle, or an essential question grabs the readers' attention and hooks them into wanting to read about the topic. See Figure 6.6 for some exciting samples of hooks.

Introduce the Reading Selection

Get great ideas from the following list when planning pre-reading activities.

- Preview the material. (See "Essential Questions" and "Brainstorming.")
- Develop and strengthen incomplete background information.
  - Give a lecturette containing the new information that is needed.
  - Use charts, graphs, posters, and pictures.

Figure 6.6 Effective hooks

Article Hooks	Literary Hooks	Artistic Hooks
Props	Mystery words	Videos or CDs
Costumes	Quotes	PowerPoint presentations
Magic tricks	Articles	Musical selections
Experiments	Headlines	Recordings
Puzzles	Riddles	Songs or raps
Mystery boxes	Poems	Cheers
Treasure chests	Stories	Musical instruments
Letters	Passages	Photographs
Artifacts	Essential questions	Paintings
Maps	Jokes	Statues
Pictures	Editorials	Role playing
Posters	Comic strips	Character debuts
	Writing activities	
	Charts	

- Correct any misconception or inaccurate facts from the brainstorming.
- Connect new topics or subjects with the readers' prior knowledge.
- Make predictions to link the prior knowledge to the reading purpose.

Examples:

What do you think the story is about?

What do you think will happen in the story?

- Explain purposes for reading the passage.
- List standards, skills, and concepts to teach in the lesson.
- Challenge inquiring minds by posting essential questions.
- Connect new information to the reader's world.
- Teach the new vocabulary words.

    - Demonstrate the pronunciation and meaning of each word.
    - Vary strategies to teach vocabulary words and their meanings.
    - Go on a vocabulary hunt to find key words. Identify and explain how each word is used in context.

Activity: Create a Sketch

1. Ask the student to create a sketch or simple drawing to reflect important procedures, main ideas, events, or steps as the information is

presented in a passage. The sketches create a pictorial sequence and enhance comprehension.
Examples:

- Draw something you know about the information.
- Design a journal, portfolio, or notebook cover.
- Create a graphic organizer, caricature, or editorial cartoon.

2. Share the design or illustration with a small group. The student uses his sketches to teach the information.

3. Display the products on a chart or poster.

4. Write 2–3 sentences as captions to explain each picture.

5. Share the pictures and captions with the class.

6. Display the pictures in a class gallery.

Set the Purposes for Reading

Establish the purposes for reading assignments in the initial planning. The reader needs to understand the purpose for reading specific information before he begins the reading assignment. The purpose sets the reader's focus on relevant information, stimulates background knowledge, and creates meaningful connections to prior learning.

Give the reader clear, concise statements to set the purpose. Use the following phrases as guides to set the purpose for reading assignments. Examples:

To learn about	To apply specific strategies
To connect old and new knowledge	To apply vocabulary terms
To locate main idea, concepts, and details	To learn structure
To use the facts on a diagram	To understand the author's purpose
To understand procedures and directions	To answer essential questions

Establish a Note-Taking Procedure

Choose a procedure to take notes of the important facts to remember. The Dual Note Organizer (Figure 6.7) and Burrito Note Taking (Figure 6.8) are two examples for taking notes. The reader takes initial notes while reading the selection. The reader then adds to those notes later during note review, discussion, or a rereading of text.

Figure 6.7   Dual Note Organizer

Notes During the Reading	Notes After the Reading

Figure 6.8   Burrito Note Taking

Text Reading Notes	Class Discussion Notes	Study Notes

Burrito Note Taking

Fold a paper in three-column folds like a burrito shell. This form makes an interesting, productive journal for the student. The reader takes notes during (1) independent text reading, (2) class discussion, and (3) independent studying.

DURING READING: THE PASSAGE VIEW

A teacher guides a student to be successful and effective as he reads. The reader must know what to do to understand the information as he reads independently or with others. The goals are for him to understand and retain the needed information in memory for later use.

An Eye on Content

Teach students to use the following strategies while reading an assignment. Model the steps for them to use as they read the text. Display the steps on a chart as a reference tool.

1. *Focus on the purpose:* Follow the directions for the assignment by carrying through the procedures and goals of the assignments.

2. *Search for cues:* Use visual and context cues. Read the headings and the subheadings.

3. *Place yourself in the scene or passage:* Imagine yourself as a part of the scenario. For example, if the passage is about an object, the reader pretends that he is an observer standing near the object.

4. *Self-correct:* If a word or phrase does not make sense, correct it. Fluent readers often self-correct automatically when a word is read incorrectly.

5. *Question yourself:* Find the key points and supporting details. Use self-questioning or self-talk as a guide during the reading of the selection. Examples:

   - What is this paragraph telling me?
   - What information do I need to remember?
   - What is the main idea?
   - What are the details that support the main idea?
   - How can I use this information?
   - What is the author saying?
   - What do I need to write in my notes?
   - How am I going to remember this information?
   - Do I need to highlight, star, or circle some facts?

Spotlight On Signals (SOS)

The author places key words and phrases as signals in a passage to assist the reader in understanding the information and to interpret his meaning. Teach the reader to recognize the signals using sticky notes or a highlighter as the spotlight. Here are some examples. Add ideas to each list.

More Is on the Way

also	and	another	first of all	furthermore	in addition
last of all	likewise	next	second	too	

Where Oh Where Can It Be?

above	across	around	behind	below	beside
east	far	here	inside	next to	right

Important Thoughts Are Coming Up Soon

a key feature	a major event	a primary concern	above all
especially important	most of all	pay attention to	remember

Two Things or Concepts Are Compared or Contrasted

also	and	but	either	like	opposite
or	rather	still	then	while	yet

Order, Order, Order

after	before	during	earlier	first	later
next	now	o'clock	then	until	while

The Author's Examples Are on the Way

for example	for instance	in the same way as	much like
similar to	such as	to illustrate	the following

Quick Changes for Thoughts

although	but	conversely	despite	different from
on the contrary	rather	the opposite	yet	nevertheless

Activity: Designs from the Mind

Teach the student to use his mental pictures or schema after reading. Teach him to use the ideas in "Designs from the Mind" as memory hooks. Model the strategy so the student knows how to use this valuable memory tool to retain and retrieve text information.

1. Read a short selection.

2. Draw a picture depicting important parts remembered.

3. Read the next passage and add another picture.

4. Continue the reading and drawing process through the selection.

5. Think about the sequential pictures created.

6. Use your illustrations as guides to discuss the information with a partner.

7. Find similarities and differences in the illustrations.

Marking the Key Points

Color-coding categorizes and processes reading information. The purpose is to identify key words, ideas, and details. Teach selective highlighting and underlining using color-coding. Adapt the strategy to the content area. Use the strategy often in lesson units, so the student knows how and when to apply it in their note taking. Here are some suggestions:

1. Highlight all adjectives that describe a key word, character, event, or situation.

2. Highlight all verbs in the passage that describe actions or movements of people or objects.

3. Highlight key words.

4. Color-code:

   - The cause with one color and the effect with a different color
   - Steps in a procedure, using a different color for each step
   - The sequence or steps in directions
   - Categories to sort and classify

Sticky Mini Tabbing

A student will enjoy cutting sticky notes into smaller, mini tabs. As he reads a passage, the tabs are placed under or above key words or phrases.

1. Assign a reading passage in the content area or supplementary text.

2. Give the student sticky notes to use as tabs.

3. Design the tabs with symbols to fit tasks from the following examples. When the reader knows how to apply the strategy, encourage him to create his personal tabbing key.

Examples:

I understand.   * (star)

I can explain.   ! (exclamation point)

I do not understand.   ? (question mark)

Variation 1: Tracking My Comprehension

a. At the end of each line of reading, the student rates his comprehension using the following symbols:

   < = I do not understand, but I can go back and figure it out in my own way.

   ? ? = I need extra help with this information.

   > = I understand this information, so I am moving on.

b. Read the selection individually and tab it.

c. Meet with a partner or a small group and discuss it.

d. Compose "What Was Learned" and "Want to Know" lists.

e. Ask the student to tell a classmate about his findings.

Variation 2: Symbols for Self-Monitoring

GVI   Got a Visual Image

RA   Read Again

☺   I Got It!

MBI   Must Be Important

LAP   Look At Picture

?   I Am Confused

Shape Up

The Shape Up strategy focuses on the main ideas, details, and key words. The student actively engages in thinking while using this strategy. It is similar to the color-coding technique and can be beneficial in student assignments in all content areas. Apply this strategy with notes daily or periodically. Students use their notes from a unit of study.

1. Draw a rectangle around each important fact to remember.

2. Select three of the ideas inside the rectangles.

3. Share the three ideas with a partner.

4. Circle the ideas the partner shares that are different.

5. Discuss similarities and differences.

Variation 1

1. Use exclamation points on the key ideas.

2. Use question marks when you have a question.

Variation 2

1. Use rectangles on the key ideas.

2. Use circles on the key parts that are questioned.

Rereading

Reread the text or topic information. During subsequent readings, the words become easier and comprehension improves. Vary the rereading strategies when it is beneficial to read the passages again. When it is possible, allow the reader to choose the reading design.

Reading Design Examples

Cloze Process: Reread the passage and fill in the blanks with important information. (See "Cloze Process" in Chapter 3.)

Echo: Someone reads a sentence. The student repeats as he follows the words.

Choral: Read the passages orally in unison with an individual student, in small groups, or the total class.

Partners: Assign the passages to be read with buddies taking turns.

Independent: The student reads the passages by himself.

Audio: The reader listens to a tape or CD of the passage as he follows the words.

FLEXIBLE GROUPING DESIGNS FOR READING TEXTS (TAPS)

What types of grouping work best in differentiated classrooms? On a sailboat, members of the crew work with different people to accomplish the mission. In a classroom, flexible grouping gives a learner the opportunity to work with others according to interests, ability, and social needs.

Readers need a blending of times to work alone and to work with others. Use flexible reading groups to meet the learner's diverse needs. Differentiate group designs, so each student has opportunities to work with others or alone to accomplish assigned reading tasks. The following approach TAPS into each learner's potential (Gregory & Chapman, 2002a) by allowing work with the Total group (T), Alone (A), with a Partner (P), or in a Small group (S).

Effectively blend the grouping scenarios in lessons. Plan reading sessions and adjust the assignments so individual learners retain the information they read. Use the flexible grouping designs to give the student alternative ways to understand and interpret assigned passages and related sources. According to research from the National Training Laboratories Institute (Alexandria, Virginia), students retain information when they are actively engaged in the learning:

Retention Rates for Information

Lecture	5 percent
Reading	10 percent
Audiovisual	20 percent
Demonstration	30 percent
Discussion	50 percent
Doing	75 percent
Using it	90 percent

T for Total Group Reading

Class Readings

Use the following guidelines for effective results with class readings for passages or special selections:

- Use short passages. Be selective.
- Make statements to establish purposeful listening.

    Examples:

    When we finish reading, you should know three ways to . . .

    At the end of the reading, join a partner to . . .

- Read the passage or selection.

Volunteer Readings

- The teacher asks for volunteer readers. The chosen volunteers should be confident oral readers rather than students who may not comprehend as they read orally.
- The teacher and the volunteers alternate reading passages out loud.
- Stop for discussions, questions, comments, and predictions.
- All students follow the words in the text as they're read aloud.
- The teacher models note-taking strategies so the students can make notes as they follow the words in the text.

Choral Readings

Use choral reading as a novel activity to read information and engage all students. Practice the strategy with a poem or a passage the class enjoys. The teacher guides the process, so students properly prepare to get the best results. When a class reads in unison, a struggling reader joins in with confidence. Choose content passages that students need to remember.

Steps for Choral Reading Presentations

1. Choose the passage.

2. Select and assign parts for individuals, small groups, and the total group.

3. Discuss tones and expressions to show feelings and emotions.

4. Rehearse assigned passages.

5. Stop periodically for suggestions and interpretations.

6. Read and celebrate.

Variations

- Call on two students to read a few pre-assigned lines of the passage as a duet.
- Assign a small group to read a section.
- Ask the total class to read a section of the passage.
- Form small groups by dividing the class into front and back sections or girls and boys.
- Use multi-age groupings so struggling readers build confidence reading to younger students.

Stage It!

Often teachers use this activity in language arts classrooms to read the characters' statements out loud. Use this strategy with content information. Choose students as readers of content passages to "Stage It." Assign each student specific content passages, so they take turns reading the information. Position each reader in a chair in front of the room with his side turned to the class. Each student faces the class when he reads his part. When the individual is not reading, he makes a one-quarter turn away from the audience.

Variation Assign each student an important noun in a selection. Each time the reading relates to his noun, he reads those sentences. If the sentence is about more than one of the nouns, the students read in unison. For example, in a geography passage defining and describing various land formations, such as deserts, prairies, and mountains, each student is responsible for one noun. The student who receives the word *mountain* reads all the sentences about his word.

Teacher Voice: Read Aloud

The teacher may need to read parts of the text aloud to the student. Ask the learner to follow along word by word during the reading. At the end of a central idea or thought, ask the student to place a finger or strip of paper at the stopping point while it is discussed. This keeps the reader focused on the passage.

Readers need to hear the teacher's reading voice often as a model. Brief readings of clippings from newspaper or magazine articles and famous quotes take very little time, but the enthusiastic reading voice of the teacher often inspires a student to read more.

Tips for Read Aloud Activities

- Rehearse the reading.
- Choose material that is easy to read and understand.
- Model voice tone, expression, and pauses.
- Stop at carefully chosen points to discuss important ideas or details and to make predictions.
- Use taped versions of the passage.
- Stop occasionally to ask students to make predictions. Include cliffhanger statements to create anticipation. Example: "I like your prediction. We will find out tomorrow if you are right."

A for Alone (Independent Reading)

Provide opportunities for students to read alone. Some learners comprehend best while reading independently. Each reader selects a comfortable place and position to read. Sometimes allow the student to choose reading materials on various aspects of the topic.

Independent reading helps develop a researcher, investigator, and comprehending reader.

Benefits of Individual Assignments

Develops interest	Increases knowledge base
Works on reading level	Answers a particular question
Provides choices	Provides for specific needs
Invokes curiosity	Gives reading practice
Develops self-regulated readers	Develops pleasure reading

P for Partner Reading

Partner reading provides students with opportunities to read the selections, discuss, and process the information learned. Students usually enjoy reading experiences when they work together with reading buddies. Use an alternate reader if a student cannot read the text, so he hears the information. The partners must get along socially, and there must be a feeling of trust and respect established.

Suggested readers:

- Teacher
- Teaching assistant
- Taped version of the text
- Peer
- Older student
- Electronic reader
- Lead reader (see "Follow the Leader" for the Neurological Impress Method)
- Volunteer

Guidelines

1. Each person chooses or is assigned a partner with whom he feels comfortable working.
2. Assign the reading selection.
3. Partners find a comfortable spot that is a suitable place to think and stay on task.
4. Each partner takes a turn reading the passage orally.
5. Partners decide how they complete the read aloud session.

Dyad Reading

1. Pair a proficient reader with a struggling reader.
2. Assign stopping points for students to
   - Discuss what they have read.
   - Write information they remember from the reading and share.
   - Use sticky notes for questions about the information.
3. Tell partners to plot information learned on a graphic organizer.
   a. Share their organizers with another set of partners.
   b. Remind partners to keep the organizer until assigned to read the next part of the selection.
   c. Begin the next assignment by reviewing information on the organizer.
   d. Read the assigned selection and add new information.

Follow the Leader

This Follow the Leader strategy is an adaptation of the Neurological Impress Method originally created by R. G. Heckelman in the 1960s. Follow these guidelines to assist a struggling reader with comprehension of the content materials. Pair the weaker reader with a stronger reader.

1. Partners orally read the information together.
2. The strong reader begins the reading orally as the other student reads along with him.
3. Gradually the strong reader softens his reading voice. The weaker reader takes the lead.
4. If the struggling reader attempts to say a word or completely mispronounces it, the stronger reader says the word and completes the phrase without stopping and interrupting the flow of thought. The weaker reader continues to read with the strong reader.
5. Students repeat the process as the stronger reader's voice becomes a whisper when the weaker reader becomes the oral reading leader.

Note: This procedure must be modeled and takes practice. It builds confidence, and because of the support, the students do not feel failure and maintain their flow of thought. There are no interruptions to correct. This works. Try it!

S for Small Group Reading

Think Tank

The different members of the group assume the following roles to complete the assignment:

a. Discussion leader or captain: Keeps the group on task and makes sure the task is completed correctly.
b. Recorder: Writes the group responses.

The group appoints one member as the discussion leader of the Think Tank. He gives a signal to stop at predetermined points in the passage to ask discussion questions. The teacher provides the questions if the students do not know how to formulate questions. Anyone in the group begins the follow-up Text Talk discussion.

Text Talk

Use the Text Talk strategy with small groups to work with oral reading of selected passages. Three or four students create an ideal group. If the group is too large, students tire while waiting for a turn. They become distracted and engage in off-task behaviors. The group decides how to read the text orally using one of the following options:

Figure 6.9   Presentation choices

Role-play.	Interview an important person from the passage.	Create a computer simulation.	Create a song, poem, jingle, cheer, or rap.
Debate an issue.	Have a mock television show.	Put information on a graphic organizer.	Conduct a panel discussion.
Demonstrate a procedure.	Make a poster.	Outline the information.	Create a mobile.

- Vote
- Use a spinner
- Draw names
- The captain decides
- Volunteers

Variation

1. The teacher assigns each group a question related to a specific section of the assignment.

2. Form small groups and give each group a section.

   a. Each group reads their assignment and brainstorms the important facts and details.

   b. The group prepares a short presentation.

Figure 6.9 shows samples of ways students can present their passage to the class. Provide options for the readers that make the presentations interesting and memorable experiences.

Others

- Be a tour guide and walk them on the journey through the passage selection.
- Have a reenactment.
- Construct a diorama.

As the group makes the presentation of their reading passage, it may be used as a performance assessment. This shows what the group or individual knows about the information in the assigned passage.

Figure 6.10 After Reading Choice Board

Summarize the big idea and put it to a beat.	Make written predictions based on the information. Share it with a partner.	Draw the sequence of events on a timeline.
Condense information and create an advertisement, banner, or slogan.	Reflect on how the information relates to your daily life.	Write the summarized information in a genre of your choice.
Combine or "chunk" chosen ideas on a chart. Illustrate it.	Plot information on a graphic organizer.	Select the most important information to create a newsflash.
Organize information learned on a semantic map.	Reflect on the significance of the information in a journal.	Create a way to remember this information.

AFTER READING: THE PASSAGE REVIEW

After reading the content material, provide time for the student to mentally process information. Model each strategy to teach the student how to use it correctly.

The reader needs to know how to apply reflective thinking strategies as he reads. Self-questioning is a strategy that has been found to have the greatest effect on reading comprehension (Rosenshine, Meister, & Chapman, 1996).

After the reader completes a reading experience, he needs various ways to make personal links and connections to the information. He must know how to apply comprehension strategies to identify and understand key concepts and main ideas.

After he learns how to clarify meaning, compare and contrast details and ideas, summarize, and form opinions, he needs to select memory strategies to retain the information. The After Reading Choice Board (Figure 6.10) provides the reader with opportunities to practice the comprehension skills and strategies.

The Passage Review

Discuss

Comprehending readers discuss what they read to process the information. They interpret ideas, analyze, and identify how the information can be used.

Search

Search for information to generate questions. Look for answers to questions similar to the following:

- What did I learn?
- How do I link what I already know with this new knowledge?
- How will I use the information?
- What parts of this passage do I need to remember?
- When or where will I use this information?

Repeat

Write the key facts and details in a unique, personal format. Repeat the information over and over until it can be remembered accurately.

Paraphrase

Recall the information or fact and give his own interpretation by saying the learned information in his own words.

Create Metaphors and Similes

Make links and connections with something familiar. Metaphors illustrate comparisons or contrasts.
Example:

The interstate was a gray ribbon winding through the mountain.

Similes use the words *like* or *as* to illustrate comparisons or contrasts.
Example:

The meteorite was like a huge ball of fire.

Rehearse

Make information meaningful by providing readers personal choices of modalities. Use your favorite memory technique to remember the information.

Chunking

Chunking is the act of grouping information to make one item, such as the causes of World War I or vocabulary words. Information is retained when seven chunks are introduced together. Chunking is the reason a person can look up a phone number in the directory and remember the number to dial it. This places the number in short-term memory. If it is a number that is dialed frequently, the dialer starts to memorize the number.

Activity: Peer-to-Peer Teaching

In the peer-to-peer activity, the reader teaches relevant, important facts and details found in a passage. The student's knowledge of the information is evident in the presentation as he expresses information in his own words. This activity generates deeper thought processing. As a result, more information enters long-term memory. As the reader prepares for this activity, he develops a deeper understanding while analyzing and summarizing the information for the teaching experience. Peer-to-peer teaching may take place with students in the class or in another grade level. A weaker reader may participate in peer-to-peer teaching with an older student. If the reader is strong, he may become a tutor for a student in a lower grade.

Form Opinions

Honor opinions. Students can journal their opinions or use graphic organizers to reflect them. A PMIS chart (see Figure 6.11) offers suggestions in the categories Pluses, Minuses, Intriguing elements, and Suggestions that students can use to fit each learning situation.

Summarize

Bring all the important facts and thoughts together in a summary as the closure. Use the information to draw a conclusion and respond to the essential question.

Figure 6.11 PMIS chart

Pluses +	Minuses −	Intriguing	Suggestions
I like _____. I agree that _____. I'll remember__. I am going to use_____.	I do not like _____. I disagree with___. _____ should be changed.	I am still thinking about _____. I think _____. I am not sure about _____.	Next time we can _____ I wish the author would _____. This would be easier if _____.

Fact Sort

1. Assign a selection to read.
2. The student writes 2–4 important facts (skip lines) from the passage.
3. Form small groups to compile facts. Cut the facts apart.
4. Sort and categorize.
5. Consolidate and rewrite similar facts.
6. Delete repeated facts.

ABC Grid

The ABC Grid (see Figure 6.12) gives the student a strategy or process to organize and collect important facts and details from content information. It offers boxes for students to record (A) the main idea of their reading, (B) details to support the main idea, and (C) facts about B. Guidelines for using the ABC Grid are as follows:

Step 1. The Teacher Models It

1. Select or assign a content passage to read.
2. Give each student a blank ABC Grid to use to plot his information.
3. Provide color-coding tools such as pens, markers, highlighters, or tiny stickers.
4. Assign a color to each step. Examples: A = red, B = green, C = blue
5. Model the steps on the overhead projector, a dry erase board, computer, or a poster so that the students can observe the teacher filling in the ideas and details from the reading in the appropriate boxes on the grid. Students complete their individual grids as the teacher modelt it.
6. Describe each step in your "Teacher Thinking" process to explain the procedure.

Step 2. The Students Practice It Independently

1. Assign a short selection from the content passage for the student to read individually and fill in the ABC Grid.
2. Provide time for each student to share his results with a partner.
3. Call on volunteers to share their results with the class.

Note: Continue to assign small selections for ABC Notes until the strategy becomes automatic for the learners. Apply this strategy in all subject

Figure 6.12 ABC Grid

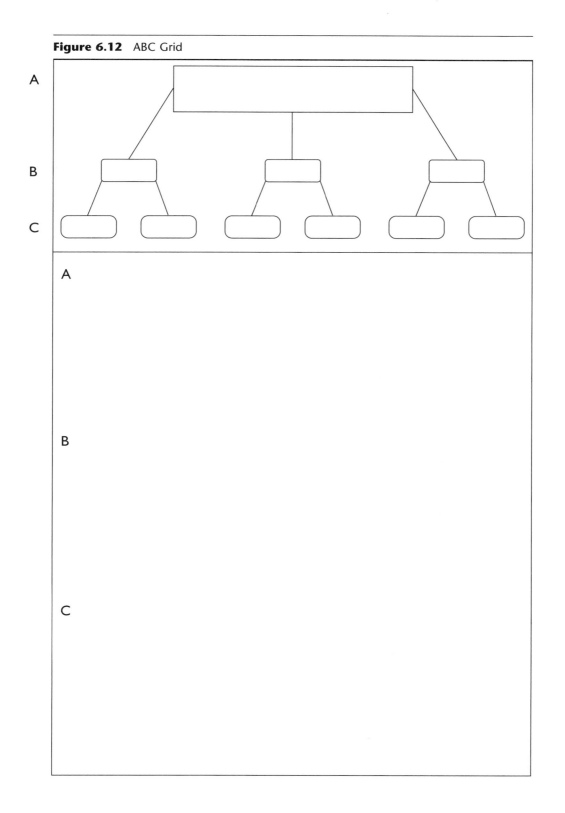

areas. Model it and apply it to various situations, so learners see how it becomes a useful tool.

Star Clusters

The purpose of this activity is for the students to select facts from their reading and organize them on a grid. This strategy teaches readers how to organize main ideas, details, and supporting facts. Use a different strip of paper for each important fact.

1. The teacher chooses a topic from the reading and writes it on a large strip of paper as the topic heading. The teacher keeps this paper throughout the activity to use as a topic organizer.

2. Each reader writes an important or "star" fact from the topic on a long strip of paper.

3. Ask each student to find one person who has a linking fact.

4. Students with linking facts become partners.

5. Linking partners find another set of partners who have facts that link.

6. Challenge these partner sets to find another linking group to form a "star cluster."

7. The three linking partner sets stand together.

8. This group develops headings on paper strips for the linking facts.

9. Students stand in position with their facts around the headings for a class discussion.

10. Each student tapes his fact strip on the topic organizer held by the teacher under the topic heading.

11. While placing the strip of paper on the grid, the students explain why the facts are in this position.

Making Beats

In this activity, music is a memory hook that stirs emotions and sets the scene.

1. List the major scenes in the selection.

2. Choose appropriate background music for each scene.

3. Make tapes or CDs with short music selections in the order they would play as the background music for a movie.

4. Role-play the main event with the musical background setting the scene.

Misfit Nonsense

A *malapropism* is a word out of place, misspelled, or similar in meaning to the needed word. The reader must use his comprehension skills to find and correct the nonsense error in each sentence.

Examples:

- He drank soda pots at the game.
- Many students were absent because of a weasel epidemic.
- She couched the basketball team.
- Jim was the first butter in the game.

Think-Pair-Share-Reflect

This activity provides time for students to process information after reading a passage.

1. *Think about it!* Ask students to think independently about the important parts, situations, procedures, steps, rules, facts, or questions in their reading. Instruct them to jot ideas down.

2. *Pair it!* Each student reads his own ideas and discusses his thoughts with a partner. Each individual shares and compares his ideas.

3. *Share with a group!* Brainstorm and discuss ideas with the total class or small group. Make a class list, chart, or organizer from the discussion.

4. *Reflect!* Select key points from ideas learned. Jot the ideas on sticky notes. Display the reflections. Teach students to use reflection statements similar to the following after reading a passage:

Examples of Reflection Triggers

- *Aha* (The most important thing I learned . . .)
- I want to learn more about . . .
- Questions I have about this subject are . . .
- How does this information relate to my life?
- What do I like about this topic?

- What have I read, studied, or experienced that relates to this information? How?
- What is the hardest part of the passage to understand?
- What do I like least? Why?
- What was the most interesting information I learned while reading the selection?
- What do I need to remember about this topic?

Response Journals

Journals are excellent tools to use when processing information after reading. Here are some effective ways to use journaling activities. These ideas and others may be used to create a Journal Choice Board.

- Write a summary, a critique, or a conclusion.
- Draw a symbol or a picture to symbolize the learning. Explain why or how the symbol represents the object or idea in the reading.
- Choose a popular song as a theme. Explain why it matches the topic.
- Write a cheer for a topic or character.
- Design a reward certificate, a medal, or an ad for the group or person studied.
- Pretend you are living in the setting. Write a letter from that viewpoint.
- Write a metaphor or analogy or use other figurative language with the information.
- Compare an individual in the unit of study to an animal.
  Example: _____is like a _____ because _____.

- Compare a setting to a familiar place.
  Example: Living in _____would be like being in _____ because_____.

- Compare an event to a happening today.
  Example: When that happened, it was similar to _____ happening.

- Create a cartoon or caricature.

Boxing Solutions

A Boxing Solutions Grid (see Figure 6.13) allows the student to reflect on essential questions or problems, predict conclusions, describe procedures for reaching solutions, and summarize solutions and conclusions.

Figure 6.13 Boxing Solutions Grid

A. Problem or Essential Question	B. Prediction	C. Procedure	D. Solution or Conclusion

1. Fold paper into a trifold.

2. In the A box, state the problem or essential question. In the B box, predict the conclusion.

3. In the C box, write the step-by-step procedure for the problem.

4. In the D box, write the solution or conclusions drawn by working the problem.

Enjoying Genres and Formats

Use different genres to analyze comprehension and promote further reading on a particular subject in the content area. These sources spark students' interest.

Teach students to use various genres and formats as a part of their reflection exercises by placing the topic information into a selected form. This is a valuable thinking activity because readers use information learned and apply it in a new way. Provide students with the following genre and format choice list to demonstrate their comprehension:

Sample

Advertisement	Grave marker	Police report
Advertising brochure	Job application	Program guide
Bartlett's quotations	Joke	Pun
Book review	Legend	Rhyme
Catalog	Letter to the editor	Riddle

Certificate	Magazine article	School notice
Comic book	Menu	Science fiction
Diary	Movie review	Short story
Drama	Mystery	Song lyrics
Fairy tale	Newspaper article	Speech
Folk tale	Persuasive essay	Travel brochure
Game rules	Poetry	

Act It Out

Use creative dramatics (McCaslin, 1990) as learning tools. The reader's unique way of expressing himself is a tool to enhance memory. Reenact a procedure, story, event, problem, conflict, sequence, or solution by role-playing.

Examples:

- Choose a student to be the narrator, and assign individual parts to classmates.
- Assign a part to each cooperative group. Have each group act out the assignment using the information in the correct order.

Creating a Stage

The following list provides various ways to create a stage for performances. Students show what they know when given an opportunity to be in the spotlight.

- Place a sheet over a pole that is braced on two chairs.
- Cut a hole in a refrigerator box to create a performance window.
- Use an old, large-screen, television frame.
- Roll the window down on an old car door.
- Use a picture frame.
- Draw the background setting on a large piece of cardboard or shower curtain.
- Use an overhead projector that projects onto a large screen. Draw each scene on a separate transparency. Students perform directly in front of the large screen, so the characters' silhouettes project for everyone to see. Students change the transparency scenes as events in the text or story unfold.
- Use four or five refrigerator boxes.

  a. Scene 1: Paint the first scene across the front of the four boxes placed upright and side by side.
  b. Turn all the boxes (one-quarter turn) clockwise and paint Scene 2 across that side of the boxes.

    c. Continue turning the boxes one-quarter turns and painting until sides three and four display the last two scenes.

    d. When presenting the play, a student sits behind each box. When the scene changes, each student turns the box to complete the scene sequence.

Puppets

Create hand puppets from materials such as socks, bags, or mittens. Use straws, paper rolls, sticks, pencils, rulers, or tongue depressors to form the base for the puppets. Make a finger puppet from glove tips or foam balls. Design the puppet to express the look, characteristics, and feelings of a text character such as a historical figure, scientist, or mathematician.

My Talking Brain

My Talking Brain is an activity designed to demonstrate self-talk for readers. Self-talk guides questioning during the reading process. Teach students the value of this strategy before, during, and after reading.

1. Select a passage with important facts or concepts.

2. Place a sign that says "Reader" above the area where the reader will sit or stand.

3. Post a sign that says "Thinking Brain" about one foot to the right or left of the first sign.

4. Read the first sentence that contains an important fact.

5. Step under the "Brain" sign to verbalize thoughts.

6. Say to the students, "When I step under the 'Brain' sign, you hear my brain's inside thinking."

Example

READER: *Reads the title for the passage.*

BRAIN: What do I know about this topic? (I am activating my prior knowledge.) What will the author be telling me about the topic? I must predict what will happen next.

READER: *Reads a sentence with an important fact.*

BRAIN: I understand this information. This says . . .

READER: *Reads the next sentence and find important facts.*

BRAIN: This is important. I am going to remember . . .

I can remember this fact if a make a quick sketch of it.

I am going to picture this part in my mind.

READER: *Reads the next sentence with an important fact.*

BRAIN: I need to find out what this means before I read any more.

This means . . .

READER: *Reads the next sentence and interpret its meaning.*

BRAIN: This is easy. It tells me . . .

READER: *Creates a memory hook to remember this information.*

BRAIN: These terms are confusing. What kind of notes do I need to take?

I will remember this by . . .

I need to ask _____ for clarification.

Example

READER: Reads a science assignment about caves.

BRAIN: How will I remember the difference between stalactite and stalagmite?

I will create a memory hook.

Stalactites have to hold on tight because they hang from the roof of a cave. Stalagmites lag on the cave floor.

STRENGTHENING COMPREHENSION

Effective Questioning

Use questions as probes to learn what information the student knows and to identify the information he needs to learn. Use the following key words at the levels of thinking identified in Bloom's Taxonomy (Bloom, 1956).

Synthesis

compose	propose	formulate	assemble	construct	
design	arrange	organize	prepare	classify	plan

Evaluation

| select | judge | predict | choose | estimate |
| value | rate | assess | confirm | evaluate |

Analysis

| distinguish | question | differentiate | solve | diagram |
| compare | investigate | criticize | experiment | contrast |

Application

| demonstrate | practice | interview | apply | translate |
| dramatize | operate | schedule | illustrate | interpret |

Comprehension

| describe | restate | explain | identify | report |
| discuss | recognize | express | locate | review |

Knowledge

| define | list | repeat | memorize | name | label |
| record | recall | relate | tell | report | narrate |

ASSESSING COMPREHENSION

Assessment and diagnosis are essential before, during, and after the reading to plan and meet the strategic needs of the learners. Some methods are formal and others informal. Teachers teach the standards and link to assessment. It is important to know if a student comprehends what he is reading and is able to express his interpretation of the information.

The following assessment ideas are adaptations of commonly used tools to assess comprehension. The authors have purposefully made these tools quicker and easier to administer. They provide instant feedback for use in routine planning to meet the individual comprehension needs.

Oral Reading Check

A quick, effective way to check comprehension ability is to read selected passages to the student. Tell the learner to orally rephrase or summarize the passages using the important ideas. Ask him to respond to "Who, What, Where, Why, and How" questions. The learner's responses demonstrate how much the student comprehends when he hears the information.

Usually, a student who has difficulty comprehending a passage as he reads has a higher level of understanding when someone is reading aloud to him. The following are sample questions to ask after someone has read the passage aloud to the student:

1. Who were the people in the passage?
2. Who used this information in his or her career?
3. What were the important parts you remember?
4. What caused this event to happen?
5. Where did the event take place?
6. Where have you heard or used this information?
7. When did this event occur?
8. Why do you need to know about this topic?
9. How does this information affect you today?
10. How will you use this new information?
11. How would you tell someone this information using your own words?

Comprehension Checklist

This is a checklist the teacher can use to assess whether the reader's comprehension is appropriate to the learning objectives for the unit of study.

Skill	Yes	No	Sometimes
1. Discusses text meaning accurately			
2. Analyzes and predicts			
3. States author's purpose			
4. Identifies the main idea			
5. Explains character roles			
6. Understands cause and effect			
7. Recalls details and important facts			
8. Interprets meaning			
9. Compares and contrasts			
10. Summarizes information			
11. Draws inferences			
12. Others_____			

Comprehension Reflection Self-Check

This is a list the student can use for a self-assessment.

- Was I comfortable? __ Yes ___No Why?
- What can I do if I don't understand the passage I read?
- I need to focus on the passage about _____.
- What do I know about this topic?
- Do I know anything about this information?
- How will I review the passage?
- Can I discuss this passage with someone? What would I say?
- How will I use the information?
- What part of the ideas or details do I need to remember?
- What kind of organizer can I use to help me remember the facts and ideas?

My Comprehending Way: "How Do I Comprehend Best?"

Discover how an individual reader comprehends best. Conduct this assessment with one student to determine his most successful comprehension method. The student may be able to comprehend using each reading method, but a reader usually has one favorite way to learn the reading material. Use the Comprehension Assessment Checklist that follows and record the results on the Recording Grid (Figure 6.16). As the student orally reads each selection, ask questions, listen to the reader's answer, and record the results in the appropriate box.

Comprehension Assessment Checklist

1. Select four or five passages that are the student's reading level or one level lower. After the level is determined, choose passages on the same level

2. Tell the student that the two of you are discovering how he comprehends best.

3. Explain that his goal is to understand the information in each passage.

4. The student reads each selection using a different method.

   a. First selection: Read orally.
   b. Second selection: Read silently.
   c. Third selection: Adult reads to the student.
   d. Fourth selection: The student chooses his favorite way to read the selection from the three methods listed (a, b, or c).

Figure 6.16 My Comprehending Way Recording Grid

Student's Name _____ Date _____

Key

✓	Correct answer expanded
•	Correct answer
?	Partial, correct answer
×	Incorrect

Forms of Reading	Explicit Question #1	Explicit Question # 2	Open-Ended Question #3	Inference Question #4
a. Oral				
b. Silent				
c. Read to				

Student Comments:

Teacher Comments:

5. After each reading form, ask two explicit questions from the selection. For instance, if a paragraph says, "Mary has a red dress," ask, "What color is Mary's dress?" Record the results.

6. Ask an open-ended question to find out what the reader retained. Record the results.

    Examples:

    What do you know after reading this passage?

    What do you remember from that paragraph?

    Tell me what you read.

    What did this passage tell you?

7. Ask an inference question and record the results.

    Examples:

    How did the character feel?

    What do you think will happen next and why?

    What was _____ thinking?

    Describe the scene.

Using the Assessment Information

This assessment shows the learner the best way for him to read when he needs to understand information. For example, if the student comprehends best as he reads orally, he knows to read the information aloud. The results assist everyone who works with the reader, as well as the student. The teacher uses the information to strategically plan instruction so the student uses reading time effectively to comprehend this information.

The checklist is a record of the student's ability to answer explicit and implicit questions. The teacher uses the information to plan specific comprehension strategies and activities. By using this assessment tool periodically, the teacher is able to monitor and adjust instruction to meet the reader's changing needs during the year.

Running Record

This is an assessment adapted from a Reading Recovery technique (Clay, 1993).

- Choose a text and a selection of 50 to 100 words.
- Ask the student to read the passage aloud. The teacher takes notes.

Figure 6.17 Running Record Tally Form

Title of Book _____ Author _____ Page Number _____ Paragraph _____
What does the reader do when he does not know a word?
Tally each error event beside the observable behavior.

1. _____ Makes no attempt
2. _____ Asks for help
3. _____ Skips the word and continues to read
4. _____ Uses letter sounds
5. _____ Uses context clues
6. _____ Tries again
7. _____ Looks at the pictures or graphics

A. number of words _____ number of errors _____
B. words _____ minus errors _____ = _____ words read correctly _____
C. words read correctly divided by _____ no. of words = ___% accurate

Student Comments

Teacher Comments

Student _____ Date _____ Class _____
Student Signature: _____
Teacher Signature: _____

- Place a check mark by all words read correctly.
- Circle omitted words.
- Add a carat (^) for an extra word the reader inserts.
- Write and draw a line through a substituted word. Write the word the student substituted above the word in the selection.
- Write "SC" above the word if the student self-corrects.
- Write "TA" above the word if the teacher assists with the word.

Record the results of the Running Record activity using Figure 6.17. The tally reveals the student's oral reading patterns.

THE TEACHER'S ROLE IN COMPREHENSION INSTRUCTION

Every teacher in every subject area is a reading teacher. The textbook and supplementary materials provide opportunities for students to learn comprehension skills so they can apply them as needed to understand the content information.

1. *Determine "how" the student comprehends best.* Readers comprehend differently. Some comprehend more when they read information aloud, others when they read silently, and still others when someone reads the passage to them.

2. *Explore the reader's personal knowledge base* to plan lessons that link his prior knowledge to the new information. A strong, effective pre-assessment is essential. Design questions and statements to activate the student's prior knowledge related to a subject before planning lessons. As a learner relates his knowledge to the new topic, he makes personal links and connections to the new information. The information gathered varies with each group of students. Use the reader's prior knowledge to effectively plan to meet his needs.

3. *Make the content come alive for the student.* Use effective pre-reading instruction to set the tone for the reader. Provide specific, meaningful purposes for reading and pique interest using advanced organizers and intriguing hooks.

4. *Provide various materials on individual reading levels and interest areas.* Use a wide variety of resources in different genres on the reader's ability levels that are related to the topic. Encourage students to choose and recommend reading materials.

5. *Provide time for each student to learn, practice, and apply comprehension skills* with a variety of related resources. Use direct instruction for identified comprehension skills.

6. *Use flexible grouping.* Give the student opportunities to read the information with the total group, alone, with partners, and in small groups. Plan for discussions of the reading with peers and adults. Group readers in varied ways using their knowledge base on the topic, interests, or ability levels. Random groupings are effective in most classrooms.

7. *Develop self-directed, fluent comprehending readers.* All students deserve the right to become comprehending readers.

SUMMARY

In this chapter, effective comprehension strategies tools, activities, and techniques are explored to make a difference in planning for the unique differences of today's learners. Step-by-step guidelines are explained with examples for teachers to adapt to give learners the tools they need to become self-directed readers.

The assessment tools are designed or adapted by the authors for ease in administration, so the results are available for immediate classroom use to assist the reader. Teachers are encouraged to create assessment tools that meet their own readers' specific needs.

Remember that every student has the right to reach his potential as a fluent comprehending reader. Each moment of improvement changes a reader's life (D'arcangelo, 1998). It is up to you!

Pulling It All Together 7

Differentiated reading instruction creates opportunities for readers to learn strategies that will be springboards to more advanced experiences. The individual's strengths and interests are the key elements for designing these learning opportunities.

USING STRATEGIES EFFECTIVELY

The ultimate goal in using differentiated instruction is to teach the student how to use his strengths to learn strategies that can be used as tools in studying or reading. A *strategy* is a way to learn a skill (Peterson & VanDerWege, 2002). A reader is able to take ownership of a strategy when he is able to apply it automatically as needed in his life. In order for this to occur, the teacher must model the strategy. While demonstrating and explaining practical applications of the steps and procedures, the teacher verbalizes the self-talk or inside thinking that accompanies each step. The strategy is modeled in various situations. Students practice the strategy with the teacher's guidance until they are able to apply it in reading situations.

Use a Variety of Strategies

Variety is the spice of learning. Vary classroom instructional strategies so that more students will retain the information. Take a key concept and brainstorm the many ways to teach it. Everyone's brain is unique; students do not all learn the same way. The content has to be relevant and fit in with what the learner wants to learn. New learning must link with prior experiences.

Ask yourself the following sample questions when deciding which strategy is most appropriate for your lesson plan:

1. What is the skill or concept I am going to teach?

2. How will I assess information the learner needs to know?

3. What are the best strategies to use for this group of students?

4. How will I group the students to teach this strategy? Remember TAPS = Total Group (T) / Alone (A) / Partner (P) / Small Groups (S).

5. How will I assess the student's ability to use this strategy?

It is essential for the student to become proficient in multiple reading strategies and to understand a range of subject material in order to:

- Use text material and textbook tools
- Apply strategies before, during, and after reading
- Learn related vocabulary words
- Use word attack skills
- Apply context clues
- Connect prior knowledge and experiences
- Adjust to the reading level of the material
- Monitor understanding
- Know when more understanding is needed
- Adjust to personal reading needs
- Pull information from the text
- Develop related questions
- Organize information
- Create a product using the information

Design instructional strategies so that the student is successful on his level of learning.

The Multi-Dimensions of Reading

Reading is a complex skill. Consider the range of the following reading variables that are addressed during reading instruction:

Purposes:	Pleasure	Specific goals
Objective:	Relaxation	To save a life
Reading materials:	Picture books	Technical books
Complexity:	One alphabet letter	A book
Motivation:	Little interest	Intense interest
Seating:	Casual	Formal

Presentation:	Individual	Large group
Noise levels	Silent	Shouting
Engaged reading:	Individual	Choral reading

TEXT CHECK

As our students strive to become successful readers, they need to be familiar with and understand book organization.

Present the Big Picture

Introduce major parts of the text so that the student knows the location and purpose of each part. Explore and explain how to use these tools to comprehend the text. Here are lists of the most common components of a textbook and its chapters. Adapt this list to teach students their texts' format.

Textbook Parts

- Cover format
- Cover illustrations
- Spine
- Copyright page
- Dedication
- Table of Contents
- Anticipation Guide
- Preface
- Chapters
- Study Guide
- Bibliography
- Glossary
- Appendix
- Index

Chapter Parts

- Introductions
- Advanced Organizers
- Headings
- Subheadings
- Bold, italicized, or highlighted terms
- Key vocabulary
- Lists

Figure 7.1 Reading Across the Content Areas

Mathematics	Science	Language Arts
Understand mathematical terms	Locate and use sources of information	Read factual and fictitious information
Analyze statistical reports	Understand and use formulas	Read information in various genres
Follow procedures	Apply data from reading to practical problems	Reflect on learning
Understand step-by-step directions	Read directions	Plot information on a graphic organizer
Solve word problems	Gain accurate information from graphic aids such as charts, diagrams, and graphs	Read and follow directions
Interpret mathematical symbols	Read for exact meaning	Conduct research projects
Read math texts and resource materials	Organize data	Locate and use information
	Research topics	Apply information to personal life situations
		Learn vocabulary
		Take notes

- Graphics
- Summaries
- Study questions
- Review activities

Analyze Text Reading Assignments

Class time is a valuable, limited resource. Effective teachers do not waste it. (*Note:* Time spent to develop rapport or improve interpersonal

Figure 7.1 Continued

Social Studies	Music	Vocational Studies	Health and Physical Education
Read maps and geographical keys and data	Read music notations and interpret music symbols for instruments and vocal	Master technical terms, symbols, and meanings	Read biographies, articles, and Web sites
Interpret graphics, charts		Interpret recipes, training and assembly manuals	Research data
Understand timelines	Comprehend musical theory		Understand advertising, media, and propaganda techniques
Read periodicals		Read charts, diagrams, pictures, drawings, and plans	
Read main idea and supporting details for factual information	Read music history and the lives of composers		
		Gain information from main ideas and specific details to make applications	Follow directions
Perform Web searches and resource searches for investigations and reporting	Evaluate music and critiques		Learn procedures and apply them
	Learn technical vocabulary	Learn about jobs and career opportunities	
Do research projects	Read and memorize song lyrics		Read training manuals or play guides
Understand vocabulary terms of cultures and geographic information	Create new musical compositions	Use safety rules and follow written directions	
Compare and contrast yesterday to today		Apply directions for projects from journals, catalogs, and magazines	

skills is not wasted.) Every aspect of a lesson should be examined to determine the best use of the teacher's and the students' time.

Determine the value of the text information by responding to the following questions as a guideline:

Is the information . . .
- Valuable in the students academic work as a

  Standard   Skill   Concept   Strategy

- On a test?
- Valuable in the students personal life?

If the answer to all questions is "No," consider abandoning the information.

BEYOND THE CLASSROOM

Special Services for Students with Severe Reading Disorders

The learner needs extra services when his reading problems are not corrected through classroom experiences. Often, a specialist or mentor who spends extra time working with the student may reinforce or strengthen his skills. Parents must approve all special services provided for the reader.

Administrators or specialists recommend programs to benefit the struggling reader. The following services are available in most schools:

Mentors	Psychologists	Speech and Language Specialists
Counselors	Social Workers	Reading Specialists
Volunteers		Resource Teachers

Parent Conferences: Let Learners Lead the Way

More parents attend conferences when their child is leading the conference. Parent conferences are exciting occasions when the student takes a major role in sharing information he is learning. Students may share their portfolios, writing journals, projects, a special book, or other accomplishments with their parents.

Some advantages of student-led conferences:

* Learning is the focus.
* Enlightening conversations take place.
* Learners become accountable.
* More in-depth analysis of the content is used.
* Students take responsibility for explaining and sharing their work.
* More parents attend.
* Parents have a set time to be actively involved.
* Parents are provided with a special time to show interest in their child's work.
* Students are motivated by the individual attention and praise.
* Each student perceives himself as a learner.

Note: If the teacher needs private time with the parents near the close of the conference, he should be prepared to have the student work with a quiet engaging activity or an activity that requires headphones. Or, it might be a good idea to plan a special, supervised event for students to attend. Some special event suggestions include:

- Videos of a favorite movie
- Sing-a-longs
- Story time
- Play time

This allows the teacher time to conference with the parents privately.

Homework Alternatives

In classrooms today homework has become a daily routine that creates nightmares for both students and parents. Too much of the work assigned is busy work. The kill-and-drill worksheets are often long and boring. If your readers are able to complete the first five items, the likelihood is that they do not need to do all of them.

When students are unable to read the directions or understand information, parents try to help and often end up doing the work for them. It is fine for parents to lend a hand, but we do not want their "student" work. Equally troublesome is the large number of students who do not have anyone to assist them at home. When they cannot do the assignment, they become frustrated and more confused. We need to think of creative ways to confront and overcome these homework obstacles.

Make Homework Relevant

Think about giving homework a new look! Assign Evening Learning Opportunities (ELOs) so the student becomes a scavenger, researcher, investigator, roving reporter, or detective. These assignments link classroom learning with the use of information in life. For example, when learning how to read directions, have the students read several easy-to-follow recipes at home. Assignments should challenge our students' minds and be thought provoking for problem solving.

Try some of the following suggestions as alternative names for homework assignments.

- ELO: Evening Learning Opportunities
- HA!: Home Assignments
- WLE: World Learning Experiences
- HLL: Home Learning Links
- Home Play
- Home Hunt
- Scavenger Hunt
- Hot Links!
- Crazy Connections

USING ASSESSMENTS EFFECTIVELY

Effective teachers plan, plan, and further plan reading experiences using assessment data that is collected before, during, and after units of study. During lessons the data is used to monitor the progress of individuals, small groups, and the total class. The data is collected through personal notes, written tests, checklists, and observation tools. Students demystify learning when they understand their strengths and areas of need (Levine, 2002). Levine says "Kids need to know themselves and they need to know what to work on to help themselves" (page 278).

The activities provided permit students to interact with ideas. Readers are actively engaged in thoughtful activities in experiences related to the content information and resources. Multiple formats are available to entice readers within their ability range and interest areas.

Portfolio Assessment

Portfolio assessments help students, teachers, and parents monitor student progress through the learner's collected work samples. A major purpose of portfolio assessment is to engage the learner (Wolf, 1989) in the evaluation as his needs and strengths are identified.

Portfolios generate student pride in work that is seldom manifested in other assessment tools (Stiggins, 1994).

Portfolio assessment:

- Empowers the learner with learning strategies and skills
- Increases the student's personal responsibility in learning
- Stresses self-efficacy, the "I can do!" feeling
- Teaches the student to be self-reflective
- Provides avenues for self-analysis and self-improvement
- Guides the learner to higher levels of thinking
- Teaches strategies for self-evaluation and peer critiques
- Generates genuine pride in accomplishments
- Creates showcases for success

Showcase Scoring

Teachers and students enjoy developing and using a scoring rubric for portfolios. The rubric sets the expectations for an assignment from the onset of the activity and leads to the final evaluation.

Example:

5 **Above and Beyond**
Completed more activities than those required

Completed and organized all assignments
Turned in on time

4 **On Track**
Completed assignments
Organized the work
Completed the work on time

3 **Not Quite There**
Missing 1–2 pieces
Few pieces organized
One day late

2 **Thrown Together**
3 or more pieces missing
Little organization
Two days late

1 **A "No Show" Effort**
Did not try
Few examples of ability
More than 2 days late

The Grading Dilemma

The biggest problem in grading in a differentiated classroom is how and when to assess the student. Often a teacher thinks, "If the student is working on his own level, then I am meeting his needs, and his grades are very high, usually A's and B's." This is the right picture because it acknowledges and celebrates growth, but it's the wrong picture if the work is below grade level. The other way to view this dilemma is that teachers must teach to state and federally mandated standards. Teachers are required to prepare students to meet those standards. Thus some of the student's grades should reflect how he is doing in comparison with the rest of the students in his grade level and at his age level across the country.

Combining Assessments

In the differentiated classroom, there must be a combination of assessments so that a true picture of the student's performance is given in the final grade. If not, all students could earn high grades, or those students who make gains but remain below grade level would still earn low grades. Try this combination of assessments:

1. *Assign grades that reflect the reader's accomplishments and areas of need.* Student efforts, creativity, and ability to stay with a task is considered in

the grade. If a reader is graded using a perspective that does not focus on his strengths, the teacher does not have a true picture of his ability. A reader's preference for learning has a major impact on his success with a concept or skill. When the reader's ability is below grade level, use an assessment tool to gather data using his strengths. For example, if the reader has difficulty with structural analysis and his strength is in the musical rhythmic area, have him create a jingle, rap, or rhyme and use it as an assessment tool.

2. *For a formal assessment, administer the same pre-test and post-test to determine the reader's growth from the learning.* This assessment is often given to the same group of readers. The results reflect his ability at the beginning of the study and his progress during the study. It also identifies his areas of strengths and needs so they can be used in planning for the next unit of study.

3. *Administer assessment pieces on the reader's grade level to compare his ability to other students in the class.* These evaluations show the reader's standing in relation to classmates. This shows how he meets the criteria or standard set for that grade level, class, or subject. Assessment is formal or informal throughout the learning. In the end, the evaluation is the grade with the portfolio showing the work.

When the teacher combines these three forms of assessment, a true picture of the reader's ability is revealed. The final grade is assigned with a portfolio as evidence to support it. This provides a more complete view of the reader's accomplishments, weaknesses, and growth. In the words of Rona F. Flippo (2001, p. 178):

> The real common ground includes the understanding that reading is not simple, and there are no simple answers or solutions that can be applied to all children and situations: Instead of simplistic answers, solutions, and one-way-only approaches, the common wisdom of the field point to the need to allow teachers the flexibility to select the methods, approaches, and materials to fit the particular child and situation.
>
> Reading development and instruction is far too complex and involves far too many variables to try to simplify and prescribe it for all children in all situations.

CONCLUSION

Teachers need to think about where they fit in making a difference with optimal learning experiences in their state, county, school, or classroom. No matter what the role, educators must join in the common goal to help every student learn and become a productive, self-directed reader. Embark upon this challenging quest by establishing a personalized curriculum through differentiated instruction.

The power of reading lifts an individual above his socioeconomic background, leads him to a chosen profession, and promotes successful experiences. A teacher who empowers a student with the reading skills and strategies he needs has given him a gift that endures for a lifetime.

Every teacher is a teacher of reading.

—W. S. Gray, 1937

DIFFERENTIATED INSTRUCTION IS LIKE A SAILBOAT RACE

On the day of the important sailboat race, each vessel is equipped with needed gear. It is in tiptop shape. The crew is ready. The goal is set to win the race. Every crew member is assigned to tasks that they do best. Excitement and cheering is heard all around as the blast is heard for the race to begin.

The sailboats follow a planned course from start to finish. Along the way, the captain and the crew revamp plans as needed. Everyone knows and follows the guidelines to avoid penalties.

The journey for some sailboats is smooth. Others have obstacles that stand in the way of victory. Although all vessels do not win the prize, the captain and each crew member learn from the experience, so they will be prepared for the next race.

Like the captain and the crew of the winning sailboat, differentiated instruction assures success for all students so that they become self-directed learners in control of the route on their reading journey.

Your goal is to create readers who are self-directed, productive problem solvers and thinkers. Differentiated reading instruction is the key.

—*Bon Voyage!*

Bibliography

Allington, R. L. (2002). You can't learn much from books you can't read. *Educational Leadership, 60(3)*, November: 16–19.

Alvermann, D. E., & Hagood, M. (2000). Fandom and critical media literacy. *Journal of Adolescent & Adult Literacy, 43*, February: p. 5.

Association for Supervision and Curriculum Development. (2002). *Reading in the content areas video series.* Alexandria, VA: Author.

Bandura, A. (1997). *Self-efficacy: The exercise of control.* New York: W. H. Freeman. Bauman, J. F., Hoffman, J., Moon, J., & Duffy-Hester, J. & A. (1998). Where are teacher voices in the phonics/whole language debate? Results from a survey of U.S. elementary classroom teachers. *Reading Teacher, 51*, 636–650.

Bean, T. W. (2002). Making reading relevant for adolescents. *Educational Leadership, 60(3)*, November: 34–37.

Bloom, B. S., et al. (1956). *Taxonomy of educational objectives. Handbook 1: Cognitive domain.* New York: David McKay.

Brown, H., & Cambourne, B. (1990). *Read and retell.* Portsmouth, NH: Heinemann Publishers.

Bruer, J. (1994). *Schools for thought: A science of learning in the classroom.* Cambridge, MA: MIT Press.

Burchers, Sam, Burchers, Max, and Burchers, Bryan. (1997). *Vocabulary cartoons: Building an educated vocabulary with visual mnemonics,* 3rd ed. Punta Gorda, FL: New Monic Books.

Caine, R. N., & Caine, G. (1994). *Making connections: Teaching and the human brain.* Menlo Park, CA: Addison-Wesley.

Carbo, M. (1987). *Phi Delta Kappan,* November: p. 197.

Chapman, C. (2000). *Sail into differentiated instruction.* Thomson, GA: Creative Learning Connection, Inc.

Chapman, C. (1993). *If the shoe fits . . . : How to develop multiple intelligences in the classroom.* Arlington Heights, IL: SkyLight.

Chapman, C., & King, R. (2003). *Differentiated instructional strategies for writing in the content areas.* Thousand Oaks, CA: Corwin Press.

Chapman, C., & King, R. (2000). *Test success in the brain compatible classroom.* Tucson, AZ: Zephyr Press.

Clay, M. (1993). *Reading recovery: A guidebook for teachers in training.* Portsmouth, NH: Heinemann.

Csikszentmihalyi, M. (1997). *Creativity: Flow and the psychology of discovery and invention.* New York: HarperCollins.

Csikszentmihalyi, M. (1990). *Flow*. New York: Harper and Row.

D'arcangelo, M. (2002). The challenge of content-area reading: A conversation with Donna Ogle. *Educational Leadership, 60(3),* November: 12–15.

D'arcangelo, M. (1998). The brains behind the brain. *Educational Leadership, 56(3),* 20–23.

Davey, B. (1983). Think-aloud: Modeling the cognitive processes of reading comprehension. *Journal of Reading, 27,* 44–47.

Farber, P. (1999). Speak up: Student-led conference is a real conversation piece. *Middle Ground 2(4),* 20–24.

Feathers, K. (1993). *Info text*. Portsmouth, NH: Heinemann.

Fisher, D., Frey, N., & Williams, D. (2002). Seven literacy strategies that work. *Educational Leadership, 60(3),* November: 70–73.

Fisher, P. J. (1998). Teaching vocabulary in linguistically diverse classrooms. *Illinois Reading Council Journal, 26,* 16–21.

Flippo, R. F. (2001). *Reading researchers in search of common ground*. Newark, DE: International Reading Association.

Gambrell, L. B., Morrow, L. M., Neuman, S. B., & Pressley, M. (1999). *Best practices in literacy instruction*. New York: Guilford.

Gardner, H. (1983). *Frames of mind: The theory of multiple intelligences*. New York: Basic Books.

Gipe, J. P. (2002). *Multiple paths to literacy: classroom techniques for struggling readers,* 5th ed. Upper Saddle River, NJ: Merrill Prentice Hall.

Glasser, W. (1998). *Choice theory in the classroom*. New York: HarperPerennial.

Glasser, W. (1990). *The quality school: managing students without coercion*. New York: Perennial Library.

Goodman, Y. M. (1998). Miscue analysis for classroom teachers: Some history and some procedures. In Constance Weaver, (Ed.), *Practicing what we know: Informed reading instruction*, Urbana, IL: National Council of Teachers of English.

Gray, W. S. (1937). The nature and organization of basic instruction in reading. In G. M. Whipple (Ed.), *The teaching of reading: A second report. 36th yearbook of the National Society for the Study of Education, Part I* (pp. 65–131). Bloomington, IN: Public School Publication Company.

Gregorc, A. F. (1985). *Inside styles: Beyond the basics: Questions and answers on style*. Maynard, MA: Gabriel Systems.

Gregory, G. H., & Chapman, C. (2002a). *Differentiated instructional strategies: One size doesn't fit all*. Thousand Oaks, CA: Corwin Press.

Gregory, G. H., & Chapman, C. (2002b). *Differentiating Instruction to meet the needs of all learners, Elementary edition*. Sandy, UT: Teach Stream/Video Journal of Education.

Gregory, G. H., & Chapman, C. (2002c). *Differentiating instruction to meet the needs of all learners, Secondary edition*. Sandy, UT: Teach Stream/Video Journal of Education.

Griffith, F., & Olson, M. (1992). Phonemic awareness helps beginning readers break the code. *Reading Teacher, 45,* 516–523.

Hansen, J. (2001). *When writers read*. Portsmouth, NH: Heinemann.

Harris, A., & Sipay, E. (1990). *How to increase reading ability*. New York: Longman.

Honig, B. (2001). *Teaching our children to read: The components of an effective, comprehensive reading program*, 2nd ed. Thousand Oaks, CA: Corwin Press.

Jensen, E. (1995). *Brain-based learning & teaching*. Del Mar, CA: Turning Point.

Kauchak, D. P., & Eggen, P. (1998). *Learning and teaching: Research-based methods*, 3rd ed. Boston: Allyn & Bacon.

Levine, M. (2002). *A mind at a time*. New York: Simon and Schuster.

McCarthy, B. (1997). A tale of four learners: 4MAT's learning styles. *Educational Leadership, 54(6)*, March: p. 46.

McCaslin, N. (1990). *Creative dramatics in the classroom*, 5th ed. New York: Longman.

McConnell, S. (1993). Talking drawings: A strategy for assisting learners. *Journal of Reading, 36(4)*, 260–269.

McDonald, L. W., O.D. (1999). *Visual training*. New York: Random House.

Palincsar, A. S., & Herrenkohl, L. R. (1999). Designing collaborative contexts: Lessons from three research programs. In A. M. O'Donnell & A. King (Eds.), *Cognitive perspectives on peer tutoring* (pp. 151–157). Mahwah, NJ: Erlbaum.

Paris, S. G., Wasik, B., Turner, J. (1991). The development of strategic readers. In R. Barr, M. L. Kamil, P. B. Mosenthal, & P. D. Pearson (Eds.), *Book of reading research: Volume II*. New York: Longman.

Peterson, D., & VanDerWege, C. (2002). Guiding children to be strategic readers. *Phi Delta Kappan, 38*, p. 437.

Piaget, J. (1952). *The origins of intelligence in children*. New York: International Universities Press.

Perkins, D. (1994). *Knowledge as design: A book for critical and creative discussion across the curriculum*. Pacific Grove, CA: Critical Thinking Press.

Pressley, M. (1998). *Reading instruction that works: The case for balanced teaching*, 2nd ed. New York: Guilford.

Raphael, T. (1982). Question-answering strategies for children. *Reading Teacher, 36*, 186–190.

Readence, J. E., Bean, T. W., & Baldwin, R. S. (1998). *Content area literacy: An integrated approach*, 6th ed. Dubuque, IA: Kendall/Hunt Publishing Company.

Renzulli, J. S., Leppien, J. H., & Hayes, T. S. (2000). *The multiple menu model: A practical guide for developing differentiated curriculum*. Mansfield Center, CT: Creative Learning Press.

Rosenshine, B., & Meister, C. (1997). Cognitive strategy instruction in reading. In S. A. Stahl & T. S. Hayes (Eds.), *Instructional Models in Reading* (pp. 85–107). Mahwah, NJ: Erlbaum.

Rosenshine, B., Meister, C., & Chapman, S. (1996). Teaching students to generate questions: A review of the intervention studies. *Review of Educational Research, 66*, 181–221.

Routman, R. (1992). Teach skills with a strategy. *Instructor 101, 9*, 34–37. Scheidecker, D., Freeman, W. (1999). *Bringing out the best in students: How legendary teachers motivate kids*. Thousand Oaks, CA: Corwin Press.

Siegler, R. S. (1998). *Children's thinking*, 3rd ed. Upper Saddle River, NJ: Prentice Hall.

Smith, C. B. (1990). Helping slow readers (ERIC/RCS). *Reading Teacher, 42(6)*, p. 416.

Soderman, A. K., Gregory, K. M., & O'Neill, L. T. (1999). *Scaffolding emergent literacy: A child-centered approach for preschool through grade 5*. Boston: Allyn & Bacon.

Sousa, D. (2001). *How the brain learns*. Thousand Oaks, CA: Corwin Press.

Sprenger, M. (1999). *Learning and memory: The brain in action*. Alexandria, VA: Association for Supervision and Curriculum Development.

Sternberg, R. (1996). *Successful intelligence: How practical and creative intelligence determine success in life.* New York: Simon & Schuster.

Stiggins, R. (1994). *Student-centered classroom assessment.* New York: Merrill.

Stipek, D. J. (1996). Motivation and instruction. In D. C. Berliner & R. C. Calfee (Eds.), *Handbook of educational psychology.* New York: Macmillan.

Strong, R. W., Silver, H. F., Perini, M. J., & Tuculescu, G. M. (2002). *Reading for academic success: Powerful strategies for struggling, average, and advanced readers, grades 7–12.* Thousand Oaks, CA: Corwin Press.

Terry, M. (2002). Translating learning style theory into developmental education practice: An article based on Gregorc's cognitive learning style. *Journal of College Reading and Learning,* Spring: p. 154.

Tierney, R. J., Readence, J. E., & Dishner, E. (1995). *Reading strategies and practices: A compendium,* 4th ed. Needham Heights, MA: Allyn & Bacon.

Tomlinson, C. A. (2001). *How to differentiate instruction in mixed-ability classrooms,* 2nd ed. Alexandria, VA: Association for Supervision and Curriculum Development.

Tomlinson, C. A. (1999). *The differentiated classroom: Responding to the needs of all learners.* Alexandria, VA: Association for Supervision and Curriculum Development.

Tomlinson, C. A., Kaplan, S. N., Renzulli, J. S., Purcell, J., Leppien, J., Burns, D. (2002). *The parallel curriculum: A design to develop high potential and challenge high-ability learners.* Thousand Oaks, CA: Corwin Press.

Trelease, J. (2001). *The read-aloud handbook,* 5th ed. New York: Penguin.

Vygotsky, L. S. (1986). *Thought and language,* Rev. ed. (A. Kozulin, Ed.). Cambridge, MA: Harvard University Press.

Vygotsky, L. S., et al. (1978*). Mind in society: The development of higher psychological processes.* Cambridge, MA: Harvard University Press.

Weaver, Constance, Ed. (1998). Miscue analysis to revaluing and assisting readers. In *Practicing what we know: Informed reading instruction.* Urbana, IL: National Council of the Teachers of English, p. 223.

Wolf, D. (1989). Portfolio assessment: Sampling student work. *Educational Leadership, 46(7),* 35–39.

Index